The Memory Palace of
Isabella Stewart Gardner

Mrs. Gardner in 1888

The
Memory
Palace
of
Isabella
Stewart
Gardner

Patricia
Vigderman

Sarabande Books
LOUISVILLE, KENTUCKY

Managing Editor
Sarabande Books, Inc.
2234 Dundee Road, Suite 200
Louisville, KY 40205

Library of Congress Cataloging-in-Publication Data

Vigderman, Patricia, 1942–
    The memory palace of Isabella Stewart Gardner / by Patricia Vigderman. — 1st ed.
      p.   cm.
    ISBN-13: 978-1-932511-43-7 (pbk. : alk. paper)
    ISBN-10: 1-932511-43-1 (pbk. : alk. paper)
    1. Gardner, Isabella Stewart, 1840–1924—Anecdotes. 2. Isabella Stewart Gardner Museum—Anecdotes. I. Title.
    N5220.G26V54 2007
    709.2—dc22   2006009178

Cover art: *Isabella Stewart Gardner in Venice*, 1894, by Anders Zorn (detail). Provided courtesy of Isabella Stewart Gardner Museum, Boston.

Manufactured in Canada
This book is printed on acid-free paper.

Sarabande Books is a nonprofit literary organization.

NATIONAL
ENDOWMENT
FOR THE ARTS

This project is supported in part by an award from the National Endowment for the Arts.

THE KENTUCKY ARTS COUNCIL

The Kentucky Arts Council, a state agency in the Commerce Cabinet, provides operational support funding for Sarabande Books with state tax dollars and federal funding from the National Endowment for the Arts, which believes that a great nation deserves great art.

For L.H.

PREFACE

Writing about the life of someone both long dead and flamboyant offers to be an ambiguous pleasure. On the one hand, the past is an impenetrable mystery; on the other, colorful evidence is irresistible. In the case of Isabella Stewart Gardner, the evidence even has its own institution: Fenway Court, the museum she built and filled, a very personal monument to art and to her own memory. Every year on her birthday, April 14, a Mass is still said in the chapel she installed on the third floor of that palace. I attended the seventy-ninth performance of the ritual, where I sat beside a long wooden carving that unfurls the injunction to say only good of the dead. I heard the little bells, smelled the incense; around me were prayers, responses, sunlight and quiet, the fountain splashing in the courtyard below. *Se monumentum requieres, circumspice,* said the priest. He was referring to Christopher Wren and his St. Paul's Cathedral in London, but also to the woman in whose house we were sitting. *We have to thank her,* he concluded cheerfully, *for giving us something to talk about.*

How to talk about her, though? Biography, however full of interesting and well-researched anecdote and information, is always bound within the time-line of human life — the achievements and relationships duly noted, the end always known in advance. The shape of Isabella Gardner's house/museum, however, invites the visitor to circle — around the courtyard, then through the second- and third-floor rooms and galleries that open their Venetian Gothic windows to that skylit space. Fenway Court invites random lingering and also returning again and again.

To find Isabella I have accepted that invitation, and imitated that process: to make her live in my imagination I have circulated around and among her objects and her friends; I've lingered with her art in the company of contemporary artists. To draw closer to her great project and to the art she left us, even as she herself recedes further into the past, I had to find a literary form that was different from biography. I had to find a way to approach my subject that was faithful both to the mysteries of her absence and to those of my own perceptions and associations. Mrs. Gardner's memory palace, then, is also full of my own memories, and of my gratitude to those whose interest, criticism, companionship, inspiration, and assistance have helped to make this book possible.

At the Gardner Museum I am grateful to April Gymiski, Richard Lingner, Kristin Parker, Becky Robbins, and Tiffany York. My gratitude as well to the Lannan Foundation for open time and open space in Marfa, Texas. For reading, advice, and support during various stages of the project, my thanks to Christopher Jane Corkery, Honor Moore, Ethan Nosowsky, Rosamund Purcell, and Jeri Weiss. Special thanks to Christina Thompson at the *Harvard Review* for her continuing understanding of all my work, to John D'Agata for invaluable formal insight, to Lee Mingwei for dinner. My thanks to Gardner family descendants George and Jason Herrick for their time and interest, to Brighde Mullens for insouciant research facilitation, and to the editors at Sarabande Books for tactfully offered improvements and for their aesthetic commitment.

My most important reader, always, is my sister Linda Bamber, my listening ear, the tireless friend of drafts and revisions, my lifelong literary and artistic interlocutor.

What is due to Lewis Hyde goes well beyond this small volume; looking forward to even further debt, I dedicate it to him anyway.

—Patricia Vigderman
Cambridge, Massachusetts

Part One

C'est Mon Plaisir
Inscription over central entrance portal

I know a few things about Isabella Stewart Gardner, but it's hard to feel really close to her. I've been to the house she built, now the Gardner Museum, on the Fenway in Boston; I've seen the art she bought and what she left behind when she died. The problem is not simply that her Boston was so different from my own, occurring as it did more than a century earlier. And it's not as if I have any difficulty with her sense that art is a lot of what makes life worthwhile. The Gardner Museum, just up the road from Boston's Museum of Fine Arts, is a lovely counter-institution created by one person to hold in perpetuity her particular sense of our relationship with art, and the relations among the artworks themselves. She wanted visiting her collection to evoke pleasure, to affect those who saw it the way she was affected.

Maybe that's just where things begin to go a little off for me, because visiting the Gardner is a mixed experience. The art is displayed in room after beautiful room, most of them opening onto a glass-covered, light filled courtyard. As visitors we are invited to relax in this airy space, to take our ease with the art, and yet the organization of that art is directed by private references and associations that often cause unease. Her great Titian is hung over a swath of patterned dress silk; a portrait by a follower of Tintoretto is high over a doorway; a row of smaller paintings are hung one over the other, seemingly with no regard for how difficult they are to see, or how the light strikes them (or doesn't); a small treasure is propped on a table so you have to crouch uncomfortably to see it; and other furniture is crowded with small aesthetic objects as if they were shells or beach glass, souvenirs of long ago outings. Moreover, none of this can be rethought, rehung, rearranged; her dead hand decrees that to disturb this little universe would be to lose it forever. It's as if Isabella's collaboration with the art is the only one going on. Eager to participate wholeheartedly in the pleasures of her legacy, you encounter imperiousness and eccentricity.

Courtyard, with Persephone

When this nouveau European palace, derived from architecture that rises beside the Grand Canal in Venice, rose itself in the urban wasteland across from Boston's marshy Fenway in 1902, it was a breathtaking display of self-assertion. The Boston Fens were and remain a testament to the ingenuity of Frederick Law Olmsted in turning a stagnant wetland into emerald parkland, but they are not the Grand Canal; their waters and reeds, lawns and gardens have not been honored by Isabella's inward-turning monument, with its palazzo façades surrounding its own interior courtyard. To step into its world is to meet a legacy of luxury and willfulness, aesthetics inextricable from personality. She put this here so that her life, her pleasure, her living presence would stay on where she put her foot down, no matter that her literal remains would end up in a family tomb in Mount Auburn Cemetery in Cambridge. What she loved, who she was, what all this meant: fragments shored against ruin.

Art stands against time and waste, against difference and indifference; it asks for my living eyes and imagination, my transient flesh. Once, wandering among art made in my own lifetime, I encountered a man whose opinion it was that you need to spend enough time with a work of art so that it can look back at you. Later, in the library, the author of a book of aesthetic philosophy confided that only after an hour of looking does a painting begin to yield him its meaning. I too am a slow looker, and I am in the habit of trusting art. Here, though, what's on offer is not just about the art. It's also a woman's refusal to disintegrate, to allow the accidents and accumulations of her life to slip into the past. When I come to Isabella Gardner's pleasure I am yielding to the lure of overturning impermanence. Her palazzo invites me to deny her absence. Entering a world whose beautiful particulars are also alien, I am yielding as well to its demand for a piece of my life. To give some of my time to what was hers is to become a part of her biography, and to bring her into mine. Trying to overcome the sense of distance and difference is to spar with change, and with the perceived finality of mortality.

I began my quest for her lost time slowly, then, with the three formal biographies that appeared at roughly forty-year intervals after her death in 1924. This turned out to be a useful window on the genre of biography, but in all of them the main character remains just that—a character, in a story someone else is telling (and from book to book, the someone else gets further and further away in time). Then I started looking at some of her travel journals and letters to people like Bernard Berenson and Henry James; I found a novel that contains a character possibly modeled on her, by Francis Marion Crawford, who was possibly the grand passion of her life. I tried to get to know some of her women friends, and what it was like to be a woman in post-Civil War Boston, and then what kind of artistic adventures the men she knew were having. I was trying to sneak up on her, but I also kept going back to look at her collection, to stand in the rooms of her museum. Troubled by the overflow of her personality (what was *I* doing *here?*), I was looking for new eyes with which to see—a new sympathy with the lost past. I turned to a friend of her later years, Okakura Kakuzo, who brought to her ravished and ravishing collection a different, and gentler, relationship to the desire for impossible permanence. Finally I turned to artists who have made this world of present-past speak in their own art.

Now my own Isabella, my own nineteenth-century world, my own fragments, have been mixed with hers. My language alone is carrying the story now, the digressions and details of my days spent in hers: my objections and discoveries, the places where I am surprised or tickled, the mysteries of spectatorship and of the irrecoverable past. All this looking and hunting is now a collection that's been my own pleasure to order and arrange, even as time carries my curious researches ever further from their object. Wandering from painting to carving to dishes to manuscripts, from history to fiction to letters and memoir, I assemble my fragments; then I enter her house, no longer a stranger.

Leaving the Paddock
Watercolor and pencil drawing by Degas in the Short Gallery,
second cupboard door (stolen)

Faced with the difficulty of penetrating a past world using the eyes of the present, historians and biographers follow the clues left behind. In Mrs.

Gardner's case, there's that huge footprint on the Fenway, but she also spent the mornings of her later years burning her personal papers so as to keep the snoops of the future from interpreting her life according to their own lights. This kind of effort to control public image inevitably invites speculation on what lies behind it. And then, if after death what's left "for the education and enjoyment of the public forever" is an immense Venetian palazzo filled with priceless works of art arranged entirely according to private aesthetic purposes, and if further specified in this legacy is that nothing in it can be changed or moved or else the whole thing has to be auctioned off in Paris and the proceeds given to Harvard College, this is just asking for gossip from the future. These were her directives; her motives, like so much about her, are concealed. The combination keeps open the temptation to shake off her will, to fill in the blanks.

The hidden past, of course, does not yield easily, not least because telling its stories also requires translating its language into that of the present. And then, the telling itself becomes part of a larger struggle to dissolve the boundaries between past and present. Entering from the busy Fenway into the quiet light of her great courtyard is deceptively simple. Finding her and her days among the works in her high rooms is elusive, seductive, frustrating—finally self-surprising.

De Absentibus Nil Nisi Bonum

("[Speak] only good of the dead") Painted wood carving, frieze from a mantelpiece (16c) in the Long Gallery

One place to search for a vanished life is in the pages of an official biography, the writings of someone accepted into that life, who breathed its air and understood its idioms. Mrs. Gardner was no stranger to gossip, and once her great project was ready for public view, she brought into the house as part of her plan to keep it in check a person she thought under enough control to do the job properly. This was her first biographer, Morris Carter. Carter knew her well for the last twenty years of her life, and wrote his book only a year after her death, in 1925. He knew the people she knew (his Preface acknowledges "the Town of Boston" as co-tellers of his tale). She appointed him as the first director of her museum, and his account is respectful and curatorial. His chapters on her travels to Egypt and the Far East use her own travel journals and letters, which is indeed interesting because you can see how undaunted she is and also aesthetically alive to the scenery. His tale has the virtue of an unobtrusive affection for her and an agreeably discreet voice; later researchers depend on him for the outlines of her story.

On the other hand, while intending to "refute some of the legends current during her lifetime" he can be annoyingly vague about such matters as why exactly "Boston society" (who? when?) was hostile to her. It's as if the idea of hostility is only colorful background for her triumphant progress—from a young bride who, not having grown up in Boston society, was an awkward addition to its sewing circles, to a woman unafraid to recommend "The Red Moon," a Negro show to which ladies could not go "without being utterly emancipated and disguised." From a reclusive young matron, to a traveler treating seasickness with champagne and biscuits. In Carter's telling, old world values bump up against new world ideals, so when his very first page announces with authority Mrs. Gardner's direct relationship to the royal family of Scotland—and possibly going back to the time of Alexander the Great—I am unfortunately reminded of the phony Duke and Dauphin in *Huckleberry Finn*.

I do understand that having an impressive lineage can be an issue, and anyway a standard way of beginning a biography is with a bit of genesis. My nearness issue really begins with a brief bit of color he can only have heard from Isabella herself, about her childhood visits to her grandparents' farm on Long Island—"periods of happiness, never to be forgotten"—that included slave children whom she enjoyed playing horse with, "using the whip on her black steeds," as he puts it, "absolute monarch" over "the pickaninnies." To read this cheerful anecdote with no further comment is to feel Morris Carter and his Town of Boston at a great and desirable distance—and this happens on page eleven. His admiration for her power does not carry across the years, and I do not travel easily with him.

A Lady in a Turban

Painting by Francesco Turbido (16c) in the Titian Room

Her second biographer, Louise Hall Tharp, wrote her book in the early 1960s. Her account opens not with the royal lineage, but with the lavish drama and glamour of the first big social event at Fenway Court, as Isabella christened the Venetian-style palace museum. Mrs. Tharp relishes this kind of event, but she is also a careful investigator, as well as in dialogue with Carter. For one thing, she explains that the field hands and house servants on the Long Island farm were *former* slaves (New Yorkers having lost what she calls slave-owning "privileges" in 1841, a year after Isabella's birth). For another, the passage of time has also made Carter's own relationship with his patron part of the story. When she first invited him to live at Fenway Court, for example, he demurred, then capitulated, and no sooner had sent his trunk but was requested to remove it as she needed the space for someone else. He did, of course, later take up residence there, and she was to him "Dea," short for *dea ex machina*, a nickname of his own unabashed design.

Mrs. Tharp goes quite deeply into the process of buying a gorgeous wardrobe in Paris in the 1880s. She has consulted the diaries of Mrs. Gardner's husband Jack as well, and has some interest in how the family's money worked. Nor is she reticent in her efforts to draw back the veil from Isabella's relationship with the young writer F. Marion Crawford. Morris Carter barely mentions this passage in her life (perhaps less insouciantly undertaken than an evening at "The Red Moon"). Handsome, a good dancer, well-educated, Crawford presented himself as attentive company for a lively woman he thought neglected by her businessman husband, but the biographer cannot overcome the shortage of real data about this intimacy. Similarly, even while quite excited to be in the company of her belle époque characters, her extensive research often does not overcome a breeziness about the actual relationships between Isabella and local luminaries such as Julia Ward Howe or Henry James.

Mrs. Gardner with Friend from the Zoo

Like Carter, she is a creature of *her* time, too delicate to mention that Isabella's most important art advisor and collaborator, Bernard Berenson, was Jewish.[1] She weaves her story as she can in the absence of burned letters, the personal pleasures of this creative intimacy spilling into the endnotes: a reference to a cousin who attended an art school that enjoyed Mrs. Gardner's patronage and thus once saw her swathed in veils; a reminiscer in the *Boston Herald* who wrote to say that when she was a child she saw Mrs. Gardner taking a lion for a walk on a leash; and finally her own experience of a golden-haired Mrs. Gardner in old age, crying out "in a voice like a parrot" to a group of visitors passing the Raphael Room at Fenway Court, "Don't touch!" In her hands the story moves along rapidly, entertainingly, but in fact she keeps her hair well tucked up beneath her turban. I find that I think of this enthusiastic biographer as *Mrs. Tharp*, as I think of her subject as *Mrs. Gardner*. They seem to be vanishing into the distance together.

El Jaleo
("The Ruckus") Sargent painting in the Spanish Cloister

Weary of biographers, and eager for more direct experience with Isabella's world, I found a book called *Interesting People*, written by a dear friend and admirer of Mrs. Gardner, Corinna Putnam Smith. Corinna was the daughter of G.H. Putnam, the New York publisher, and wife of the painter Joseph Lindon Smith, whose work you can see in the Gardner Museum and whose charming letters, often decorated with little drawings, attest to

---

1. His birth, she tells her readers, is "Lithuanian," his nose "Grecian," and the possibility of his curls being "ritualistically cut when he was thirteen" never explained.

an affectionate, fruitful, and flattering friendship.[2] (Smith was in fact Mrs. Gardner's first choice to direct her museum after her death, but as he was not available she settled on Carter instead.) Corinna comes forward with the brio of a flamenco dancer to tell us about her life in the company of important people (it's actually subtitled *Eighty Years with the Great and Near Great*). By her own account she was quite a figure in the first quarter of the twentieth century, popping up like Zelig to chat with and advise poets (Oliver Wendell Holmes), ambassadors (the British one), or the Secretary of State. During the First World War it was General Pershing,[3] then President Taft, even Winston Churchill. And lest we miss the value of attending to her conversation, she includes having called the winner

Corinna Putnam Smith and Friends

---

2. "Sitting in the rich gloom of a splendid Buddhist temple," he writes from Kyoto in May 1901, "...I often get to thinking of all the deep toned places and pictures it has been my good fortune to paint and learn to know so well, and my mind invariably runs into a pleasant channel...which leads me, in my reveries into a series of stately rooms with treasures therein displayed—and I see you the genius of the place—and I am happy in the thought that I may be of some use to you."

3. Pershing she found "the perfect type for a commander-in-chief" given his "strong face, with a good mouth and a well-formed chin, stern eyes, and a manner suggesting a determination to attend to business and not waste time." Her ability and determination to report on troop morale, to tell both him and "plain soldiers" things they needed to know "was later to cause quite a stir at headquarters."

of the 1924 Derby, a long shot who won by more than a length and a half.

On the first floor of Fenway Court, at the end of a long dim cloister to the left of the skylit courtyard, is another version of such happy confidence, a large painting of a Spanish dancer by John Singer Sargent. Framed by a specially built Moorish arch and dramatically lit from below as if by footlights, the painted dancer bending backward and raising her bright silk skirt over one firm heel, the image is a portrait of excitement. The excitement of travel, costume, female self-presentation; of a world emerging in areas of lights and darks. Pink shawls, dark-hatted musicians, guitars in the flamenco night. Drawing visitors down the quiet passageway, Sargent's painting has a youthful sense of his own power in a wider world. His Spanish ruckus comes toward us still alive, asking for our attention and company.

Corinna's self-expression, adventurous in its way as Sargent's strokes of light and dark, was focused on the idea of being socially useful. There used to be something called a "clubwoman," an upper-class woman with philanthropic and community-improving designs, who belonged to a women's organization that supported art, theater, and musical associations, medical and educational activities, social and relief work, and other civic-minded projects. This got her out of the house while still respectably within a female sphere (not, that is, into "The Red Moon"). Many of these associations were enormously effective, contributing to lasting institutions like the great city museums or women's medical colleges, while opening to women a nondomestic world.

Another side of these good works is offered by the historian Wanda Corn who adds flamboyant behavior to the pattern: wealthy women who wanted to express their independence but not to have to break with their social class adopted eccentricity as a style—"a performative mode" she says, "…used to claim cultural authority in social settings where previously they had none." For Isabella Gardner's generation nonconformity was a way of getting attention and a way of getting things done. Corn's idea puts things like that stroll with the lion in context; it suggests as well some of the thrilling presentation in the painting of the Spanish dancer.

You can also see the appeal for women in the generation immediately following, women like Corinna Smith who were both well brought up and eager to show their stuff. How they showed it, though, can be puzzling. Take, for example, her involvement with the Koran, which began, she says, because as a young woman she was once seated at dinner next to Professor Charles Eliot Norton of Harvard University, and he ignored her. She figured that the way to impress him would be to learn Arabic, which she luckily had the connections to do (an introduction to the interestingly named Professor Toy on Trowbridge Street, in Cambridge).

A Woman Representing Virtue
Marble statue (14c) in the West Cloister

One can learn a lot by reading a book like Mrs. Smith's, but I'm sorry to say it's not congenial company. First of all, there's the constant crescendo of heroic action. There seems no situation her heroic woman's voice was unequal to, from persuading strikers not to withhold supplies to troops overseas to getting the Irish in the St. Patrick's Day parade to acknowledge English heroism. "Battles are rarely won by flight," she notes helpfully, now a "full-fledged participant, by invitation" in the parade. It all makes me feel quite small and invisible.[4] The real difficulty I have in translating *this* past, the true distancing, is an effect of a narrative style so flat that no crescendo ever resolves. An extended account of a truly peak moment involves Corinna so impressing a major Egyptian Imam with her knowledge of the Koran that he took her to a noon service at a Cairo mosque. All went well at first, but when the dervishes got up to do their circle dance, their leader objected to her Christian presence, growling things like "dog of a Christian," which thanks to her Arabic skills she was able to understand. She stood her ground, even though the Imam by this time was edging away.

What this was like for her I have no idea; nor does she show us the angry Sufi. When next we see her she's in a class of young boys whom she easily surpassed at learning the ninety-nine attributes of Allah, thus making herself welcome at any noon prayer on any Friday in any mosque in Egypt. But there is no music in her impressive stand for ecumenism, no rhythm to her verbal choreography.

Corinna Putnam Smith

---

4. In later life Corinna took up social reform: the treatment of Native Americans, helping released women prisoners, opposing the growing of poppies in the US for the use of bakeries (the narcotics commissioner, another one of her confidants, told her it would result in bootlegged opium).

I've seen dervishes dancing, too, and these days some of them are women, so that the moment when they take off their cloaks and begin to whirl is cinematic, intimate, a garden suddenly coming into bloom because while the men are all in white, the women whirl in colors—dark green or blue with red, or peach, lime green, yellow. They dance with their extended right hands always palm up, left hands palm down to show that everything they take from the deity is given to the people, keeping nothing for themselves. Things have changed, Mrs. Smith, and you can't be expected to see me some eight decades down the line, ignorant of Allah's attributes, an anonymous tourist relying on a printed handout to explain what I'm seeing, but your song of risky and gender-bending religious participation is badly tuned to my hopefully listening ear.

Incensing the Veil

Sargent watercolor sketch in the Blue Room

Ah, Corinna, this hapless self-presentation as unofficial ambassador for morality, Christianity, and female intelligence isn't just your fault, and I am trying to get beyond my impatience and irony. In those days personal intimacy with the future was the last thing anyone wanted. They may have been flamboyant, but they kept a sharp eye on the audience. There was Mrs. Gardner burning her letters and who knows what else that would have been so interesting, not only about her, but about the intimacies of her vanished world. And this anxiety was not confined to women; Henry Adams burned all his wife's letters from her father after her death. Henry James traveled to Venice in order to burn the correspondence and journals of his friend Constance Fenimore Woolson after her suicide, trying to keep whatever had been between them nobody else's business, even though this kind of hard data is not indispensable for nosing out the truth, or at any rate, the story.[5]

James's fear of intimacy is famous, I guess, but you can also see his behavior as part of a tradition of self-fashioning perfectly in accord with Corinna Smith's uncongenial reticence in describing her Koranic experience, or Isabella Gardner's claim to royal lineage. Still, the effort to keep the nosy future from reading between the lines is hopeless, whether the lines are as shapely as James's, or as clumsy as Corinna Smith's. The veil itself can also burn, offering its own fragrance.

The Recording Angel

John LaFarge watercolor study in the Blue Room

Before there was Fenway Court, there was 152 Beacon Street, in Boston's Back Bay. Isabella's father bought the house for her shortly after her marriage to Jack Gardner; twenty years later, she bought the adjoining house and combined the two, thus providing herself with many more walls for her growing art collection and more rooms for entertainment. Disappointingly, you can stand on Beacon Street in front of the same address but her double house is gone; another mansion replaced it in 1904, the same year she opened Fenway Court. Indeed, it's hard to find the Back Bay of her days, created as a tremendously profitable civic improvement, the urban design derived from Haussmann's for Paris, the houses built according to the most up-to-date French form, often as

---

5. For that you need imaginative sensibilities and a talent for putting one word after another, which you'd have thought Henry James would know—but he was in a panic over privacy, and I hope of grief. According to Lyndall Gordon's biography of *him*, which has both those qualities, he also tried to drown Woolson's dresses in the Grand Canal.

investments.[6] Wealthy men already perfectly well-housed bought plots and built houses to give to family members, creating an instant context of wealthy connections. Number 241 Beacon Street, for example, was given to Julia Ward Howe by her brother Sam, making her and her beautiful daughter Maud neighbors of the Gardners.

Julia, who wrote "The Battle Hymn of the Republic" (along with a lot of poetry that has not withstood the years), was an enormous progressive and literary presence in Boston in her time. Maud adored and admired her, and finally became the family biographer. Her book, called *Three Generations*, sifts through the attic, turning up diary excerpts, letters, discarded theater programs, foxed photos, and old news clippings. Sadly, her use of these documents is not a great improvement over the burning strategy (at least for my purposes). She was a great friend of Isabella Gardner's, and a cousin to Francis Marion Crawford, but (like Corinna Smith) she is not skilled at telling me what I want to know. Her narrative retains the opacity of distance, as when an unexpected sentence at the very end of her chapter about six months spent in New Orleans offers our first glimpse of the artist John Elliott: a brief mention of her marriage to him. It's as if her intended audience were people who already knew she had married him; as if the book imagined a future that went no further than her own social world. She will not show me her romantic cousin Frank Crawford; indeed, Mrs. Tharp says Maud protected him from Mrs. Gardner when the relationship grew too intense, and she is protecting him from us as well. That door in the attic is firmly shut.

This pretty recording angel was nevertheless active in many good causes, and she too got around at the turn of the twentieth century. She

---

6. Jack Gardner in fact built seven residences as rental property on nearby Marlborough Street.

Maud Howe Elliott

and her husband lived for many years in Rome, where she was correspondent on Italian affairs to several American papers. But like Morris Carter she is always part of that faraway Town of Boston, an abolitionist's daughter who fantasizes (surely in jest?) of purchasing a beautiful Nubian to bring home to a friend. "Do you remember," she quotes from one of her own letters, "Constance Rothschild's Nubian and how faithful he was to her?"

Clearly it takes a defter hand than hers to manage the intricate relationship between aesthetics, politics, and affection. Her friend Henry Adams, who manages the intricacies quite deftly, is a provocative contrast, but in his *Education*, she says, she was surprised not to find the man she knew. How, asks this upper-class community improver, could someone who had achieved "an enviable distinction in [his] day and generation" confess himself "woefully disappointed with life"? There was that unfortunate suicide of his wife, of course, a person who has no place at all either in *Three Generations* or in *The Education of Henry Adams*, but, as I'm saying, Maud was no gossip.

We are about as welcome, it seems, in the private lives of the past as Corinna Smith in a mosque. We may learn their language and the names of the gods they worshipped, and perhaps be admitted to Friday noon services. In their autobiographies, however, they do not seek to make our acquaintance.[7] To know them and to like them, we have to be free to digress, to circle around them, to pick up what pleases us. To be intimate with the world to which Fenway Court was finally presented, I have had to make voices other than Isabella's speak to me. Like her slow gathering of the art collection that became her life's work, my search for her will travel far from its moorings before finding its home in the chilly Boston spring.

Study of a Young Lady Reading
Lithotint by Whistler in the Short Gallery, third cupboard door

In the Short Gallery on the second floor of the Gardner Museum is a series of four large cupboards, designed by Isabella herself to hold her prints and drawings. These are on movable panels, like those in a poster display. As a visitor you are invited to pause in your exploration of this place. The Short Gallery is crammed with paintings, including a flamboyant portrait of Isabella herself by Anders Zorn, her arms spread wide, long pearl necklace falling below her waist, the dark Venice night behind her through the open window, and a less flamboyant one of her by Martin Mower, standing in

---

7. Corinna Smith relates an anecdote about a "little school teacher" from Worcester, Massachusetts, "eager to improve herself" but first driven from the Titian Room by Mrs. Gardner because she was taking notes and later invited back for lunch. She imagines this humble beneficiary as one of many "insignificant people" whose "drab existence" her friend Isabella improved. What indeed am I to think of my own note-taking, even though today the guards kindly offer pencils, should you be carelessly jotting in ink?

feathered hat and spotted veil, her eyes inclined toward a large book in her hands. There are also portraits of her mother and her husband, along with a cabinet of many interesting objects, but if you have the patience to linger and leaf through the heavy panels in the drawing cupboards there are surprising glimpses into the collection: a drawing by Michelangelo, and one by Raphael, five by Matisse. There are also dozens of prints by Whistler—a small image of two sisters in conversation, for example; another of a young woman reading. Whistler's women here are having their lives, we are catching them when they are not on display. That is how I want to go back in time, to those moments of private thought and being, and so I am beginning with the absent Mrs. Henry Adams, elided by her husband in his most famous work, but speaking in the fragments that remain of her voice in a language that draws me closer to her time.

She was known as Clover, born Marian Hooper in 1843—three years later than Isabella Stewart Gardner. Her story offers another vantage from which to look at Isabella's world, since she came out of the same social gene pool, although she grew up just outside of Boston (on the North Shore) and didn't marry so young. Her biographer Eugenia Kaledin sees her as making an effort to be deliberately different, but in her case eccentricity was not just a style; it was part of a more complicated birthright. Her mother and aunts, closely associated with Margaret Fuller's female translation of Transcendentalism, saw freedom from convention as a unifying spiritual force—not just a way to get out of the house. Thus when Clover heard that her cousin Annie Hooper, the daughter of a Congressman, had been politically discreet in the social presence of secessionists, she protested such holding of her tongue: "in the presence of Gomorrah...I should think spontaneous combustion would have ensued."

By the time she met Henry, she had learned German, Latin, and "alas,

I fear," as he put it to an old college friend, "a little Greek, but very little." He was nervous about what his friends would think of her—at that point, at least, her intelligence being a kind of secret vice he enjoyed in private. Their marriage began with a honeymoon in Europe and Egypt. Like others of their class they were tireless travelers, and the trip up the Nile was full of encounters with other Americans and English. Clover's letters, like Isabella's travel journals, mention encounters with a cast of characters by this time familiar to me from my reading: the Sam Wards (that generous Sam who gave Maud's mother her house; uncle as well to Frank Crawford), a Mr. Roosevelt from New York (accompanied by the future President, who was fourteen at the time), the Gardners, the Emersons. Ralph Waldo Emerson, possibly to his credit, felt his ignorance of this exotic locale a perpetual humiliation on his Nile trip. (Corinna Smith, on the other hand, was able to turn the awkward discovery of a stowaway on their hired *fellahin* to her advantage, compelling him to teach her correct Arabic pronunciation until he fled the boat one morning before she was up.)

Form and Manner of Keeping the Parliament of England

Manuscript written for Edward VI (1547) in the Long Gallery

Now, Clover, as it happens, can put one word after another in an entertaining way, so her letters have some bite to them. They are mostly to her father and don't say much about her personal life, but you can still see a person there— a person and a marriage. In Clover's unconventional family democratic principles were entwined with their witty conversation, and one interesting thing about both Henry and Clover is that, unlike so many in their world, they were no Anglophiles (the *Education* in fact is a reminder that for the

Adamses the English were the historical enemy). Clover was not blinded by the eager welcome they received in grateful memory of his father's service as American ambassador, or by the forms and manners of British ceremony. "The lowest of Dante's hells," she observed, "must hold an English table d'hôte.... When the animals are all collected, the head waiter bangs on the table with some heavy instrument, and the inevitable clergyman says grace." (As a child of Transcendentalism, Clover would naturally not have respect for this institutionalized God.) "Then comes a very nasty dinner which the hungry, silent Briton prolongs for one hour and a half. Then the waiter bangs again, and a perfunctory thanksgiving follows. Even a fanatic," she adds, "cannot express gratitude for an English breakfast, and it is happily omitted." The specificity of these scornful opinions resonates out from Isabella's world, Americans not so dazzled by the trappings of ancient nobility that they lose their engaging wit. Details like her disgusted account of the small ratty hotel rooms favored by the British (an economy that allowed them to dress their footmen, she says) keep me with her—bringing her life into mine.

A Young Lady of Fashion

Painting on wood by Paolo Ucello (15c) in the Long Gallery

The Gardners and the Adamses were friends in Europe—Isabella introduced Clover to her favorite dressmaker, Worth, a visit to whose studio was a sort of theatrical event. Skeptical about the fuss, Clover was nevertheless delighted when the first gown showed up: It "not only fills my small soul," she admitted, "but seals it hermetically."[8] Leaving an English soirée together,

---

8. After a while she gets rather bored by the prospect of new clothes, but goes on ordering them, for "Henry says, 'People who study Greek must take pains with their dress.'" Henry was an aesthete and an ironist; you can see that it would be a pleasure to have a wife you can say something like that to.

Mrs. G. and Mrs. A. stood together in the vestibule waiting for their broughams (pronounced like "brooms" but meaning a particular kind of horse-drawn vehicle appropriate for conveying ladies dressed in Worth gowns around town), and entertaining themselves with sartorial and socio-logical observations. "Down come an elderly female in black, followed by a jolly-looking, very fat one, and the Britons fall back on either side and bend their sovereign-loving knees, because it's the Grand Duchess of Mecklenberg-something and her sister Mary of Teck," Mrs. A. writes to her father.

Two lively young women from Boston; a lighthearted moment in a London vestibule—Clover's observations have an irreverence that transcends the fashionable moment. Ucello's painting in Mrs. Gardner's third-floor gallery, though entirely of its Renaissance Florence, has a similar gaiety and refusal of routine piety. His young lady is bright with reds and blues and gold; hers is not the profile of an angel. Ucello is famous for his pleasure in the discovery of perspective, for his clear-minded wit. How pleasing, then, to see that spirit in another form, another century, in the colors of epistolary language.

Yet neither of these young ladies from Boston was a stranger to suffering, as it happens. Isabella had already lost a passionately loved baby son and been advised to have no more children. Clover had lost her freethinking, emotionally intrepid mother when still a child. Nor would she herself ever have a child. But in this era of the great culture raids on Europe, both plunged happily into some of the great pleasures attendant on a great raid. For Isabella Gardner, the city of her heart was Venice, where she and the indulgent Jack rented a palazzo and invited their friends to visit. The Adamses explored Paris, whose delights Clover professed herself unequal to describing or properly appreciating, but I think we can get the flavor well enough when she says, "We never dine in our hotel, but browse far and wide and can tell you the merits of half the restaurants in Paris."

A Young Lady of Fashion

Her account of a typical day has them studying and reading "peacefully" till early afternoon, then out to "mouse in picture shops, Louvre, Luxembourg, etc." before returning for tea between five and six. After which, Henry James shows up and they go out for dinner and three times a week to the theater. Friday, she says, getting to the particular, "we dined at the famous Diner de Paris, a huge place, five francs a head, wine included. If you skip a course, you can make it up in more wine or what you like." It's not noon prayer in a mosque, but it lets you see enough of the ritual that you want to be there.

A Gondolier

Black-and-white ink sketch by Vittore Carpaccio (16c)
in the Short Gallery

James was a friend of Isabella's, too, but she wasn't the kind of material Clover was. He wrote to a friend in 1880, that Clover was "a perfect Voltaire in petticoats." Meaning, I suppose, that she was witty, opinionated, and female. Like his loved cousin Minny Temple, Clover served as a model for Isabel Archer in *The Portrait of a Lady*—an "honest, adventuresome female spirit trying (perhaps with limited success) to choose knowledge, enjoyment, liberty." Clover, Minny, and the fictional Isabel Archer are made eccentric in their time by their intellect and spontaneity.[9] How attractive that is, and how useful in particular to a novelist with his own designs on the future. (Another important example: although Minny died very young of tuberculosis, she was later reincarnated as Milly Theale in the Laocoönic sentences and paragraphs of *The Wings of the Dove*.)

Despite her continuing charm for countless others—and the use of her name for the lovely and doomed Miss Archer—James never found Isabella Gardner a character of deep interest. It's not just that she was so clearly not doomed. He thought she tried too hard and listened too sympathetically; her taste was not fine enough. Yet, "how fond of her one always is," he confided to a mutual friend after visiting her in 1907, following a hiatus in their relationship of many years, "for the perfect terms

---

9. This is how Lyndall Gordon puts it in her excellent biography *A Private Life of Henry James*, which also displays an adventuresome spirit by putting James in the context of the women whose affections and openness served him so well as literary material. (For this latter-day eccentricity Gordon was rewarded with bluenosed critical disapproval.)

one is on with her, her admirable ease, temper and *facilité à vivre.*" Of all the things I've read, this remark gets me closest to her, even with the little lapse into French around the tail. She, too, was a bit of a guilty pleasure, for this high aesthete, at least.

A Gondolier

James's presence at the edges of Isabella Gardner's story (an oarsman silently listening, with his own purposes) is important to my story because his writing (for all its interminable circumspection) imagines me. His digressing sentences are written for the eyes of the future, and just so do they transcend the distance I feel from the less artful Corinna Smith and Maud Elliott. James may not have wanted me to see his letters to Constance Fenimore Woolson, but his fiction leaves the attic door unlocked. He doesn't prohibit the touch of my imagination on his world.

A Woman Threading a Needle

Dry point by Paul César Helleu in the Short Gallery

I am free, for example, to see in Isabel Archer a dilemma suffered by Clover that arises in a very different form for Isabella. Clover, too, created an appealing social space around herself—she was a Washington hostess of considerable skill—but both birth and marriage kept her aware of her inferior educational status. Her feelings about her education she compared to being in a dory without oars. She had been sent to the Agassiz School for Girls in Cambridge, where the curriculum included plenty of math, science, and languages ancient and modern. (Thus her own practical pleasure in language itself.) Meanwhile, just down the road Harvard's President Eliot pointed out that "the world knows next to nothing about the natural mental capacities of the female sex," and perhaps because of this perplexity Harvard was reluctant to allow women to use Harvard Yard as a thoroughfare to get to the library. Apparently it was easier for a camel to go through the eye of a needle than for a woman to make her way into the kingdom of books.

Another route to education was attachment to an educated man, someone with the franchise to lounge around all day in the Yard if he pleased. Henry Adams supported women's education, although he felt it was in general detrimental to their emotional lives. Nevertheless, he continued to enjoy his secret vice, trying out his writings on Clover, "on the theory that she is the average reader." She seems not to have shared his contempt for his own education.

Isabella's educational path seems less emotionally thorny. She was sent to private parlor schools run by respectable ladies in New York, then to a finishing school in Paris, then taken briefly to Italy (she was very good at the necessary languages for this). Shortly thereafter, she married the brother of an American friend she had met in Paris. Jack Gardner was a jolly young businessman with a lineage that connected him to American history as firmly as Henry Adams's did. The Gardners were a branch of the Lowell family, whose kinship network was rooted in New England's eighteenth-century mercantile fortunes. Neither his political awareness, however, nor his erudition were anything to intimidate a lively woman. For her education Isabella relied on extramarital conversations, one inspiration being Corinna Smith's rude dinner companion Professor Charles Eliot Norton, whose lecture series on art she attended in 1878, and whose Dante study circle she later joined. Such friendship allowed her to develop a taste for art and literature and collecting without the trouble of learning Arabic.

Jack Gardner

In due course she found younger men, wonderfully educated and generally artistic, with whom to further develop her interests. Bernard Berenson and Francis Marion Crawford are the most significant for the story, the former for his role in forming the art collection now in the Gardner Museum, the latter for the way he perhaps absconded with her heart. Also Joseph Lindon Smith, who sometimes signed his letters "Joe-rinna" to indicate his affection was shared by his wife, and who went to considerable personal trouble to get the fresco painting of Hercules by Piero della Francesca safely from the wall in Borgo Sansepolchro on which it was painted to one in Fenway Court. Such a pleasant lifelong learning

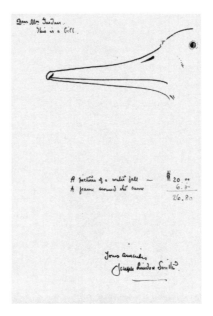

Letter from Joseph Lindon Smith,
May 9, 1903

situation supported by a generous husband and the continued creativity of Worth may be more likely to foster a *facilité à vivre* than the single companionship of an aesthetically inclined historian like Henry Adams whose own autobiography discusses himself in the third person.[10]

The Tragedy of Lucretia

Painting on wood by Botticelli (16c) in the Raphael Room

On the other hand, it's hard to dismiss a marriage of true minds, particularly since that mousing in the picture shops and the Luxembourg gardens, the browsing in half the restaurants in Paris, doesn't sound exactly stifling. Clover's letters show her life with Henry unfolding very agreeably. She seems to be the one who connects more readily with other people, the one willing to trot out her rudimentary Spanish for a family sharing their train compartment on the way to Seville. Indeed, her translingual adventurousness both got them into the National Archives there, and allowed her to chat up the archivist while the shyer Henry searched for what he needed. Later, when they got to Morocco, she was able to arrange for them to be served partridge instead of "a dinner of garlic and waste messes" by explaining "that we were Americans and that Americans if possible wish to eat partridge on Wednesdays." These are not negligible skills, as any traveler will recognize.

Missing, perhaps burned by Adams following her death, is any anecdote that might whisper suicide. Even so, her mother's sister Susan Bigelow, and eventually her older sister Ellen were suicides. A cousin died in the Somerville Asylum; her father, who gave up his own medical

---

10. "Why is the coffee at your house so much better than other people's?" Maud Elliott once asked Mr. Gardner. "Because we are very extravagant," he replied. "The only way to have good coffee is to buy the best, and use a lot of it."

practice to care for his motherless children, volunteered at the Worcester Asylum for the Mentally Ill. Maybe just as interesting as the genetic story is the lifelong awareness, the admission into consciousness of mental instability. You can see how attractively this would play for Henry James, shading her eager liveliness like a long, elegantly turned parenthesis.

Oh, it's well for James to attend to the unacknowledged dilemmas of women's souls; the mystery of female being makes great subject matter for a male artist. In one of the Gardner Museum's Italian rooms is a panel painted by Botticelli telling the story of the virtuous Roman wife Lucretia, threatened with rape by Sextus Tarquin precisely because of her exemplary chastity. Rembrandt, Titian, Veronese, Ovid, Dante, Livy—all had a go at her story. As Livy recounts her words to her husband after her forced submission: "As for me, I am innocent at fault, but I will take my punishment. Never shall Lucretia provide a precedent for unchaste women to escape what they deserve." Whereupon she stabs herself and dies. Here in Isabella's Raphael Room, on a wall covered in red silk damask, Botticelli's image is a series of tableaux, the scenes linked by the architectural mise en scène. On the left Lucretia is threatened by Tarquin; on the right she falls, after killing herself. In the center, over the bier where she lies with the dagger in her heart, an energetic Brutus incites a dozen or so Roman soldiers to rise and expel the house of Tarquin. Arches and columns frame the figures, receding in a theatrical demonstration of linear perspective. (In the room light falls across the parquet, shaped by the courtyard window into Venetian Gothic counterpoint to classical drama.)

The story is dramatic, and its consequences brought about the establishment of the Roman Empire, but in this painting the elaborate architecture with its detailed decorative reliefs commands more attention than the stage business of its little figures. The dead Lucretia is almost lost in this telling, a woman who turned her valor against herself.

The reasons why a woman in late nineteenth-century America might turn against herself are perhaps not so hard to imagine; the distance between feminine expectations and achievement are still with us (although Lucretia's singleness of mind is a particularly enraging precedent). Mythic images of female possibility and female appeal are everywhere, entangling themselves with ordinary spiritual and social aspirations. Another of Mrs. Gardner's Botticellis, on the floor above, is much less stark and easier to read: a tender image of Madonna and Child with an angel beside them holding grapes and wheat. The sculpture-like presences with their breathtakingly beautiful faces and downcast eyes express an insistent ideal of female perfection. One strong hand supports the baby's thigh even as the other touches an ear of wheat, His future body. The combination of beauty and seriousness of purpose is both inspiring and daunting.

The Adams Dogs Taking Tea

Clover and Henry rode their horses in the lovely lingering Washington fall days; the window boxes under their study windows were gay with roses, blue daisies, and nasturtiums on Clover's side, while in Henry's their four

33

small dogs took their ease. Real life offers this kind of plain sweetness, the photograph of the dogs taking tea at a little low table. Along with her other talents, Clover was a photographer, a creator herself of images, adept with her machine. She turned it on her father and husband, on the loved housekeeper who cared for her as a child, on the dogs, on the heroes both male and female of her time. She mastered the demanding complications of nineteenth-century photography, but in the end she turned to the chemicals of her art to poison herself on a Sunday in winter.

Among the Rocks

Painting by Howard Gardiner Cushing in the Blue Room

Even Henry James's careful probing beneath the surface of things does not quite explain how even a woman determined to seize life for herself might avoid the rocks of convention and self-doubt. When his Isabel Archer is finally stricken to see that the whole shape of her life has not been her own vision, but rather as she has been used by others, *the truth of things*, James says, *their mutual relations, their meaning...rose before her with a kind of architectural vastness. She remembered a thousand trifles; they started to life with the spontaneity of a shiver.*

In the novel it's a moment of horrifying awareness, a construction of her life from which his heroine cannot escape. In Clover's story, however, in Maud's, in Corinna's, I am picking up the pieces of a world still unassembled, incomplete in my perception. Isabella Gardner, too, in what ought to be a great palace of memory has spread a thousand trifles. Among them somewhere, within the architecture she herself chose, and among these bits of anecdote and memory, history and friendship and evidence that has not been destroyed, is a woman and an elusive past.

fili tirati e represi

("threads drawn and darned") Spanish altar frontal (16c)
in the Spanish Chapel

Clover Adams did not in fact like *The Portrait of a Lady,* did not like the probing style, did not recognize herself. Indeed, the lively individuality of her own language stands in fragmentary counterpoint to the silence of her underdocumented death, and her short life is itself also a poignant counterpoint to Isabella Gardner's long one. Both included unconventional marriages, mental instability, and the Civil War. Given how firmly we are shut out from what they may have said (or not said), the differences in their relationships to these events may begin to pick out patterns in the past, may begin to give meaning to the thousand trifles in Isabella's life story and to the art collection that she has left us. She is the one who endured, whose life and legend emerge from the nineteenth century in a way that Clover's cannot. Unworthy, perhaps, of James's fictional attention, she offers her own creation to ours. Her museum continues to invite a pulling together of the broken narrative threads.

For Isabella, mental instability and the Civil War coincided in the early years of her marriage, when she was transplanted from New York to Boston, a change that even today would represent a lowering of the social temperature. Her new family was both Brahmin and mercantile, putting her into some pretty drab company and also as it happens into a peculiar relation to the war, thanks to the Gardners's trading interests in the South, and the consequent risk to the ships sent to bring the cotton they needed for their mills. Biographers can't avoid her assertion that she was too young to remember the Civil War, which is clearly not true literally. Clover, three years younger, was passionately interested in the war and went to considerable trouble in May of 1865 to find a man who would escort her and three female friends from Boston to Washington to see the Grand Review of Sherman's and Grant's armies. But if you were a young woman in a young marriage, a young woman negotiating a Back Bay recently reclaimed by extravagant enterprise from the tidal flats of the Charles River and designed as a neighborhood for the city's elite, a young woman whose husband paid for a substitute to fight for him in the war, and a young woman whose only child was born and died during the conflict, your youth might indeed have been a time when a great national upheaval passed you by. Which doesn't address the issue of a middle-aged woman lying about her age, but it does reflect an ability to keep renewing oneself in difficult circumstances.[11]

The Coronation of Hebe

Ceiling painting by an assistant of Paolo Veronese (16c)
in the Veronese Room

In Isabella's case, as in Clover Adams's, the causes that explain staying or going lie all around, unassembled into plot. Meanwhile, historical forces seen or unseen, grasped or ignored, entangle themselves into the unwinding narrative. Conversions are always mysterious, and the conversion to art is full of chance events, uncharted influences, peripheral causes. The pieces of the story, its characters and subplots, shift as the light of imagination changes. We see these lives in fragments and shape them to our own.

---

11. I don't mean to be apologizing for her. How bad is it not to be engaged by a major national political event? Not to feel some stake in the outcome of a war being fought in your own country? On the other hand, how bad is it not to be able to vote—or to walk through Harvard Yard, for that matter?

Like childbirth, war is very dramatic while it's going on, but its importance is reframed by what the subsequent years make of it. In Boston the end of the Civil War brought both expanded industrial wealth and an influx of (increasingly organized) industrial workers. Waves of immigration, which would enlarge the city's population more than twentyfold in the course of the century, threatened to create a political opposition to Brahmin hegemony. A solution to this identity crisis was a quietly engineered cultural war, at the end of which high culture had successfully seceded from low entertainment. Art lends itself freely to many purposes, and here the development of cultural institutions like the Museum of Fine Arts and the Boston Symphony Orchestra offered a way to foster the tastes and values so useful in giving an upper-class identity and solidarity.

For Isabella Gardner the aftermath of both war and childbirth was finally the death of the child in March of 1865, three months short of his second birthday, and debilitating depression for her. The family doctor suggested a trip abroad. The story is that she basically had to be carried onto the ship on a mattress, she was so weak; six months later she returned in excellent health and spirits with a trunkful of beautiful clothes from Paris and an awakened interest in music and art that became the passion of her lifetime and the fuel that warmed her experience of Boston's chilly social scene. She missed the war, but she did not miss the next big moment.

On the contrary, in fact: she used it to her own ends. To begin with, she made herself into a bit of an artwork—showing up in yards of silk draped closely around her body when the other Boston ladies were still in hoops. Daughter of merchant capitalism, wife in a major textile industry family, and possessor of a slender, curvy body, she entered the cultural economy in finery that demanded attention and homage. "Pray, who undressed you?" inquired a gentleman encountering her on the stairs at a ball, expressing—in the way of gentlemen confronted with something unfamiliar and sexy—both admiration and anxiety. "Worth," she replied; "didn't he do it well?" She didn't have Clover's irony, but she did know how to turn a punch line. And she treated Boston's artistic institutions with similar (perhaps calculated) insouciance. She surrounded herself with young writers, artists, and musicians, promoting with her patronage and friendship contemporary rather than anointed art.

The Message to the Woodcutters
Flemish tapestry (16c) in the Gothic Room

Fenway Court certainly has its share of anointed art—and seems at first viewing very much an artifact of the past—but it was conceived and built for the immediate enjoyment of art, rather than for the moral education and uplift on which the city's upper class based its aesthetic stewardship of the Museum of Fine Arts. While fights at the museum erupted around the mission of educating taste, Isabella's message, and her last word about high art was "C'est Mon Plaisir," the motto over the front door of her museum.[12] The issue of how the public was supposed to look at art remained a concern, however, for the men who had entwined their financial power with a cultural style that established them more and more firmly as an upper class.

By 1906 the Museum of Fine Arts was a well-established Boston landmark, and its board took very seriously the mission of educating public

---

12. It is true that when she came to dedicate her museum to the public, she imagined their pleasure would be similar to hers, and was unpleasantly surprised to discover both how very numerous it was and its impulses to remove souvenirs. Rules, guards, an entrance fee eventually made enjoyment of the art a more exclusive privilege than the wording of her will might imply.

taste. In the first part of the nineteenth century it was common for copies of European masterworks to be commissioned and displayed for the edification of the raw American public (after the Civil War, as more Americans were traveling to Europe, they became of less interest). Still at the MFA was a collection of plaster-cast reproductions of the famous works of marble antiquity, an established and respected presence. That year, though, a war erupted over the value of these copies. The young acting director of the museum, an Englishman named Matthew Prichard, thought they were hideous, and wanted to get rid of them.

The Plaster Casts

By that time Fenway Court too was a Boston landmark, and Prichard, as it happens, was a close friend and protégé of Isabella Gardner, who also thought the casts had no role in the cultivation of pleasure in art. So although her female voice was never invited to speak in the board rooms of the city's cultural institutions, her opinion in this case was very much part of the winning side. The institutional disagreement ended bitterly in the defeat of the old guard, and the resignation from the board of one of her oldest friends, William Sturgis Bigelow.[13]

Although Prichard left the museum not long after the plaster casts, his portrait remained in the Macknight Room at Fenway Court. In due course Bigelow returned to Mrs. Gardner's luncheon table, and she continued as part of the artistic hegemony of the city's upper class, while remaining in close touch with Prichard and following her pleasures where they took her. She lived among her lovely painted Madonnas and tapestry landscapes — not in them — and the Town of Boston was always free to read about her in the gossip pages: that promenade with the lion from the zoo, or the private boxing match organized in an artist's studio for herself and several women friends (she was in fact a great sports fan).

The Shower of Gold

Painting by Howard Gardiner Cushing in the Blue Room

This all sounds delightfully unconventional and lively, and that is certainly the press on Mrs. G. She went her own way, she associated with whom she wished, she traveled the globe, she surrounded herself with attractive young men, and she assembled a glorious art collection. I do find this appealing. At the same time, the combination of out-of-sight social entitlement and female undereducation still distances me from Isabella and troubles my perception of her museum. I am also a fan of pleasure in general, however, and female unconventionality in particular, so I'm not

---

13. The larger issue here is how the public was supposed to look at art, and whether these imitations were effective in the formation of aesthetic taste. Today such objects are curiosities, but the question they raise is still alive: when we look at art, are we supposed to be learning what's considered good or developing our own powers of perception, our own sense of the past? And contemporary art education would be difficult without slides of the great works of the past.

giving up yet on the search for nearness. And indeed, written very near to me in time is that third biography of Isabella Stewart Gardner.

Disappointing as my previous encounters with biography have been, I am still looking for one that will help me pull her out of the awkward past. *The Art of Scandal*, by Douglass Shand-Tucci, does offer to do just that. Looking at her from the vantage of the 1990s, he sees a woman for our own time. Rather than flouting proprieties, he says, she was acting as a liberating force, someone with "an instinct for social freedom."

Shand-Tucci's Isabella is pro-gay, feminist, racially inclusive, a friend to all outsiders. He even tries to make her out as having had abolitionist sympathies, and suggests that had she lived in our time she'd have been called a "fag hag." His biography appeared seventy-three years after her death, but he seems to have solved the nearness problem; it's clear that his relationship to her is very close—and the more he looks at her, the more he sees what he likes.

This shower of praise, unfortunately, applauds eccentricity and intimacy to the point of fawning on celebrity. A belated member of her circle of young aesthetes, he finds only flattery in one critic's suggestion that Isabella Gardner's waistline is the model for Charlotte Stant's in Henry James's *The Golden Bowl*. He quotes with pleasure from the Master's fictional world: "the extraordinary fineness of her flexible waist...which gave her the likeness also to some long loose silk purse, well-filled with gold pieces, but having been passed empty through a fingering that held it together." To me this reads like insulting sexual innuendo—as close as James might come to a snigger at the freedom, the perceived looseness, Isabella enjoyed in her marriage. (Of a piece, perhaps, with the guilty pleasure he took in her company, that *facilité* he discreetly masks with French.)

Shand-Tucci sweeps away James's carefully constructed language; for complexity he substitutes a gusto expressed in multiple exclamation points, uncovering the gay and racy world of her young associates. His extensive research, however, turned up no suggestion of important erotic high-jinks on her part other than the relationship with Crawford, which he takes very seriously.[14] Any hint of a dark side, in other words, is missing from this joyful account by Dea's latest conquest. It's all thrilling, and all perfectly available to him.

Once again I am in the company of a biographer whose excitement and admiration I cannot share, no matter the urging of his exclamatory style. He has gone neck and crop for a version of Isabella Gardner and her legacy that suits his particular taste. Fenway Court, for him is "a brilliant example of Modernism's key technique of collage," an immense installation for invited guests, a "dialogue between Old World Decadence and New World vitality." His breathless art criticism reframes the museum in a language of celebrity; looking back with approval to Morris Carter's defense of Isabella's artistic vision as not to be tampered with, he finds the way she "persuaded works of art to relate to each other and to the viewer... life enhancing."

The transformation of Isabella into someone whose sociological impulses would be entirely congenial to us today is as uncongenial to me as his uncritical acceptance of Fenway Court. That she was a woman with great gifts for both friendship and the continual refreshment of spirit is clear, but her idiosyncratic education also gave her an aesthetic confidence that while compelling is not necessarily infallible. A twist of the kaleidoscope can make visiting her museum feel like an experience of collecting mania, an example of an enthusiastic spirit on holiday in an

---

14. "Deeply, passionately intimate" is how he describes it, and indeed feels close enough to his imagined and long-dead lovers to illustrate with an experience of his own what he means by intimacy.

auction house. Thirteenth-century stone lions from Verona and Venice. A Roman sarcophagus carved with maenads and satyrs in the third century. A Spanish silver sanctuary lamp from the seventeenth century; cups, mirrors, chopsticks, coins, altarpieces; velvets, silks, and lace; wooden guardian animals created to ward off evil spirits from a fifteenth-century Japanese Shinto shrine; a fireplace canopy with the coat of arms of Queen Isabella of Spain—the one whose generosity gave Columbus three ships with which to pursue his own dialogue between the old and new worlds. Shand-Tucci's relationship to all this is little help in sorting through them, or in finding my own way in this past.

Retable in North Cloister

If I am to share her biography and her pleasure, submit to her will and still move easily in her rooms, I will have to step back from the golden shower of her acquisition. Some of the things I love here are the least showy, like the French limestone retable in the North Cloister, carved so delicately and improbably into scenes from the Passion. Someone in the fifteenth century took the time, had the patience and skill, to bring out of the stone these lively, intricate little figures, the terrible story made astonishing again by the care with which the anonymous artist wielded his tools. Or, once, turning my head by chance as I climbed the stairs from the second floor, I

43

was suddenly facing a bit of a fresco by Giorgio Vasari in which four musicians seem to be leaning out a window from sixteenth-century Florence just across from me, an unexpected delight that now I look for every time I pass. Or the painting in the Blue Room called *The Omnibus*, by Anders Zorn, a painter I'd never heard of before I came to this museum. It's kind of a portrait of the pretty passenger who is closest to me, but in the receding diagonal composition—the man napping beside her, the one in the top hat a few seats away, the one partly cut off by the edge of the painting—she does not offer herself to my gaze. She's just there, going somewhere one day in the nineteenth century.

These are the things that make me want to know Isabella, and to know the friends who helped her satisfy her pleasure, spend her gold. The upside of Shand-Tucci's exuberance is the way it reminds me of her openness and generosity, for it was Isabella's talent for generous friendships that brought her the services and education of a less scattershot aesthetic confidence, one that brought to her the Botticellis, for example, and many other of her collection's great works. In her relationship to Bernard Berenson—the man who invented connoisseurship—was the opportunity to refine her own aesthetic gusto.

Indeed, Isabella's relationship both to Berenson and to his wife Mary is a large fragment of her enterprise, albeit one with some jagged edges. When she met Bernard Berenson he was a promising and ambitious Harvard student from a poor immigrant family. The Gardners contributed significantly to a private fund that sent him to Europe on a "traveling fellowship" in 1887. After he published *Venetian Painters of the Renaissance* in 1894, that initial investment developed into an art-buying partnership that was foundational for both her collection and his career.

Mary Berenson, trained by her husband and an enthusiastic partner in

Young Bernard Berenson
with Curls and Grecian Nose

their work, was a skillful broker for Isabella's collection, as well as for those of other wealthy Americans. If she once called Fenway Court a junk shop of art, ravished from where it belonged, in a mellower moment she did fall in with the fashionable terminology and call it a work of genius. Her own story, as it happens, complicates Isabella's in a way that points up some limits on both women and art collecting and puts Shand-Tucci's time-traveling portrait into a different frame.

A Girl Taking a Thorn from Her Foot
Painting by a follower of Correggio (16c) in the Titian Room

Mary Berenson, a generation younger than Isabella Gardner, seems to offer a less constrained contrast to her than Clover Adams (for one thing, her family was less drawn to epistolary incineration). The brilliant, headstrong, and adored daughter in a matriarchal Philadelphia Quaker family, she was sent to Smith College and to the newly established Harvard Annex in Cambridge.[15] To her family's dismay she married at twenty-one a philosophy-loving Irish barrister named Frank Costelloe and went to live in London. At twenty-seven she left him and their two small daughters to live with Bernard Berenson; when Costelloe died nine years later they were married. Her unconventionality was less a performative strategy for cultural participation than a testimony to her family's encouragement of intelligence and agency. She knew how to act on her desire rather than suffering the pain of having stepped into a wrong spot. Beginning as Berenson's pupil in the study of art, she later shared his work, becoming an expert herself in the connoisseurship he brought to aesthetic enjoyment.

Mary Berenson in 1884

---

15. Her mother, Hannah Whitall Smith, was a preacher, reformer, and writer; her sister Alys, who married Bertrand Russell, was a women's rights and temperance activist; her brother, Logan Pearsall Smith, was a well-known essayist and critic.

The contradictions of her relationship to Mrs. Gardner, to her own social world, and to the art the Berensons were steadily shipping across the Atlantic suggests a more nuanced dialogue between Old World decadence and New World vitality. Her granddaughter Barbara Strachey suggests she undertook with high spirits the circumvention of the laws against removal of national treasures from Italy, in collusion with the American millionaires on whose patronage the Berensons "life of cultured luxury" depended (both the Italian government and U.S. Customs often had opinions that conflicted with the desires of the Berensons's patron-customers). Her scholarship, intelligence, and wit, her social and organizational skills, and her resourcefulness in the face of officialdom were essential, though mostly unacknowledged, to their partnership. It was in many ways another marriage of true minds in which the woman, although far from "oarless," nevertheless felt herself the inferior. She was a generation younger than Clover Adams, but her intellectual accomplishments too were a bit of a secret vice. Indeed, Shand-Tucci suggests that in spite of Isabella's debt to Berenson's connoisseurship, what she

Bernard Berenson and Mary Costelloe

47

created was more of an individual achievement than his, precisely because of his underacknowledged artistic (and economic) collaboration with Mary.

The Triumphs of Fame, Time and Eternity
Painting on wood panel by Pesellino (15c) in the Early Italian Room

The Berensons's relationship to Isabella Gardner was about art, about Italy, and about patronage. Coming upon two painted panels by "the very rare and wonderful Pesellino" in August of 1897, Berenson writes to her of this opportunity: "…it is for you—o Lady—to buy them." He compares the artist with Giorgione, with Fra Angelico, with Masaccio. He tells her that they are "the translation into visual form by one man of genius, of the poetical creation of another" (Petrarch's *Triumphs*); that "placed one over another over a mantle, they would be perfect as furniture"; and that the 8,000 pounds she should pay for them is a bargain. Thanks to such persuasive and confident language were the Berensons able slowly to restore their lovely villa in the hills outside Florence. They became sought-after experts consulted by more and more Americans who hoped to get their wealth on the right side of the divide between elite art and lowbrow taste.

This lucrative necessity for aesthetic distinctions was an important artifact of the late nineteenth-century reorganization of American city institutions, a move designed to monopolize, legitimize, and sacralize art and music, most strikingly in Boston, which at the time was America's cultural center as well as high Brahmin fief. That's how Paul DiMaggio describes what was happening, in an article that sketches in some of the historical architecture, or at least indicates some of the *mutual relations* (to use Henry James's phrase) among my accumulating trifles. The Irish were taking over politics, and a prosperous middle class was developing—a class that enjoyed musical performances like the Railway Gallop, during which a little steam engine scooted around the hall with black cotton wool smoke coming out of its funnel.

This engaging detail in DiMaggio's article is part of his argument that the Brahmin directors of the Museum of Fine Arts and the Boston Symphony Orchestra ultimately were able to define what high art was, and to separate it from stuff like the Railway Gallop and museums that interspersed paintings with mutant animals, Chinese curiosities, mermaids, and dwarves. They and others of like mind and fortune took Shakespeare out of the circus, and between 1870 and 1900 created the institutions (including men's clubs and prep schools) that made clear what it meant to be upper class.

The city's corporate artistic institutions, that is, were modeled on the numerous nonprofit institutions already accommodating the needs of wealthy capitalists: Harvard University, Massachusetts General Hospital, the various charitable institutions. Fame may be overtaken by time, and time by eternity, but meanwhile art was becoming a status marker that didn't just launder money, it transubstantiated it—making the Berensons's expertise quite the valuable intangible and their lives inextricably connected to the very rich (who came to them for advice) and art dealers (who came to them for clientele). In the story of how Boston led the way in the creation of cultural capital, Isabella Gardner's role is often described as "eccentric"—complementary to the process, but not central. Her long relationship with the Berensons, though, suggests that her dialogue with high art is simply a bit closer to the way art once flourished as part of the same show as magic acts—the flight of doves from the battered top hat, or, in the case of the Berensons, friendship from a flight of greenbacks. And, in Isabella Stewart Gardner's case, cultural centrality from a fluttering eye for artistically promising young men.

49

"The Bamboo Announces Peace"
Chinese steatite seal (19c) in the Early Italian Room

While I do not fault the magical properties of art or the educational qualities of friendship, I am still an uncomfortable onlooker at Isabella's maneuvers in the Gilded Age art scene. Surrounded by flattery and luxury, she did expect to get what she wanted. The *plaisir* in her *C'est Mon Plaisir* means "will" as clearly as it means "pleasure," and willfulness is not really a good friend to art. So, I want to jump into the twentieth century, and the later years of her life, when her "eccentricity" led her to a different kind of acquaintance. In 1904 the now well-established Museum of Fine Arts engaged as curator of its extensive new collection of Asian art the gifted and sophisticated Japanese connoisseur Okakura Kakuzo. Okakura, who was deeply involved in the preservation of traditional art in Japan, was extensively educated in the cultures of both East and West. Well-connected in New York and Boston, he was socially graceful, physically appealing, philosophically original and serious. He was also no stranger to self-fashioning, sometimes with flamboyance, dressing as a representative of the East in formal traditional robes. In his Tokyo neighborhood he had been called the "Prince on Horseback"; he practiced the art of archery and lectured to his students at the Tokyo School of Art by moonlight. He was introduced to Mrs. Gardner shortly after his arrival in Boston.

Isabella was deeply affected by Okakura, but his relationship to her was less as an art advisor than as a spiritual and aesthetic friend. Their friendship suggests a dimension to her that does begin to draw me close. His introduction to the Japanese tea ceremony, *The Book of Tea* (written in English), was first read to an audience at Green Hill, Mrs. Gardner's summer home in Brookline, Massachusetts, in 1906. *The Book of Tea* develops the Taoist and Zen idea that "true beauty could only be discovered by one who mentally completed the incomplete," which is indeed what I am hoping to do with Mrs. Gardner. The little book both makes the principles of the tea ceremony compatible with Western ideals (such as democracy and equality) and challenges Western approaches to art.

Okakura confronted the distance between Eastern and Western thought, and believed in cross-cultural friendship anyway. In his time he was a bridge between Eastern and Western art; his thinking is also a bridge between his end of the twentieth century and ours. He invites his readers to "linger in the beautiful foolishness of things," to beatify the mundane, to be true to our individual tastes, all of which does seem to have more to do with the spirit of many artists working today than with the canonization of Old Masters that was so much a feature of his time.

Okakura Kakuzo

It is true that at the Museum of Fine Arts, as Anne Nishimura Morse puts it, he "positioned himself and his Japanese staff as the only true experts." In less than a year he catalogued thousands of paintings and other objects, and effectively made the case for calling a selection of these works masterpieces. Nevertheless, Okakura also had quite a few ideas that have not solidified into cultural institutions run by possible members of the audience at Green Hill. "Our mind is the canvas on which the artists lay their colour," he says, be they Italian or Japanese; "their pigments are our emotions; their chiaroscuro the light of joy, the shadow of sadness. The masterpiece is of ourselves, as we are of the masterpiece." This sense that the mind of the looker is a component of a work of art was precisely not the kind of idea likely to appeal to the guardians of an artistic monopoly, for whom the masterpiece, authenticated by someone like Bernard Berenson (or Okakura himself), was decidedly and uniquely of itself alone, and looking at it a way of becoming more refined. I want to try imagining that Okakura's peaceful way appealed to Isabella; that like mine, her pleasure in art was in the way its secrets become ours as we give it our attention. Its privacy is shared; we draw near and the years between us don't seem so awkward.

"A Fresh Rain Passed Over This Lonely Mountain..."

Inscription on Chinese painted enamel dish in the Little Salon

Okakura's Tang-era tea ceremony calls for tea leaves with "creases like the leathern boot of Tartar horsemen," tea leaves that "curl like the dewlap of a mighty bullock, unfold like mist rising out of a ravine," and several more now inaccessible similes. Even using the shabby equipment of the present, though, and in spite of the unimpressive kind of tea I drink, Okakura's *Book of Tea* is as alive for me today as it was in 1906; his presence in the life of Isabella Stewart Gardner offers a back door into her story, a door that is not under the motto of her imperious *"Plaisir."* The philosophy of tea as Okakura describes it is "a worship of the Imperfect"; it's "a tender attempt to accomplish something possible in this impossible thing we know as life." His little book brings a freshness to my search I have not found elsewhere.

Okakura visited Isabella at Fenway Court and at Green Hill. He brought other Japanese artists to visit her as well, and read to her poems and tales of the East in her garden. "Perhaps tomorrow night I shall see them mistily coming up over the grass," she wrote to Berenson, "the only light, their cigarette. It has really made the summer different." It made her different as well, or at least that was Mary Berenson's perception. "At last we really care for her as a human being," Mary wrote to her family in 1914, recounting their longtime patron and friend's tearful confession of former selfishness, her desire "to get rid of old evils" and her learning from Okakura to seek to love rather than to be loved.

In Okakura's cross-cultural perspective Fenway Court was not Shand-Tucci's modernist collage. The aesthetic of *The Book of Tea* is one of simplicity, impermanence, and contemplation potentially in direct opposition to the lavishness, permanence, and elaborate organization represented by the collecting style of his friend. His own conversation with her palazzo is not about old and new, decadence and vitality, but instead transforms it into an object for contemplation on impermanence: "The stars have dissolved/To make a crystal night" he wrote, describing Fenway Court, ". . . . /A shadow glides/On the stairway of jade." Neither critic nor fan, his view of impermanence seems to allow the desire for permanence, and even to acknowledge beauty in its illusion. Her pigments, that is, became his emotions, her chiaroscuro the light of joy, the shadow of sadness. In this philosophical expansion, the culture wars of the late nineteenth century lose some of their intensity, and the contradictions of Isabella's place within them feel somewhat less distancing.

Part Two

Two Warriors Gallop Across the Uji River

Eight-fold Japanese screen (17c) in the second-floor
stairway passage, south

The Asian wing in Boston's Museum of Fine Arts always seems quieter than
the rest of the museum. Never the site of blockbuster exhibitions of famous
works or artists, it inspires a kind of attention that turns in another direction.
Its treasures are in beautifully wrought or decorated glass, jade, porcelain; or
in a long scroll of painted narrative, the miniature social world both alive and
stilled; or in the astonishment of the details on a bronze dancing deity. There
is no hurrying from masterpiece to masterpiece here; pleasure has to be a
matter of attentiveness, slow gazing. In old Chinese paintings of mountains
and rivers the human presence is very small, a few monks on a path, a boat,
a cluster of fragile houses. And a spectator can relax into her own smallness,
as into the misty light over the grass and the glowing point of the cigarette.

The friendship with Okakura was Isabella Gardner's personal harvest
from another important moment in Boston's history as a cultural node,
another cultural shift she did not miss. This moment is strikingly illustrated
by the Buddha Room at the Museum of Fine Arts. Stone-floored and dimly
lit, with three very large Buddhas (one gilded) flanked by guardian kings
and spirits, this expensive interface between art and culture was designed
in 1909 to make sure that as these artifacts became designated as art in the
West they did not lose the meaning they'd had in another time and place.
Modeled on an eighth-century Japanese monastic complex, it has a
coffered wooden ceiling, stucco walls, tapered wooden columns—the
room entangles plunder, cultural openness, and spiritual longing. It's a bit
of a theme space: the great statues meditating under the swinging lamps,
the art students busy with their sketchbooks, the vaguely spiritual dimness,

the rack of plastic-coated pages explaining the figures and their signifi-
cance (legacy of the educational faction). Even the empty space feels
co-opted into the installation. Although a very different aesthetic
experience from Mrs. Gardner's installation on the Fenway, this too is an
invitation into her world. Like the museum's larger Asian collection, it is a
legacy of both the personal questing and the power of a social and cultural
elite — so much so in fact that their portraits are part of the permanent
collection (although not always on display).

Look at William Sturgis Bigelow: son of the Gardner family's
physician, he abandoned a medical career and spent most of the 1880s in
Tokyo where he became, as the museum's signage explains, "an adherent
of Esoteric Buddhism." I have seen his portrait, painted with photographic
precision by a Japanese artist on a silk scroll, hanging across from a case of
carved wooden faces taken from his enormous collection of Noh masks.
Or notice Edward Sylvester Morse of Salem, a marine biologist who went
to Japan even earlier, as that country turned eagerly to the West in the
decades after Commodore Perry opened the Japanese ports in 1853. He
went to study bivalves, and was promptly offered a position teaching at the
newly established University of Tokyo, which allowed him to introduce
Darwin to the Japanese.[16] Ernest Francisco Fenollosa, collector and cata-
loguer of Japanese art treasures, was recruited by Morse to teach political
philosophy at the university but became more interested in the preservation of Japanese art and culture; he became an Imperial Commissioner of
Fine Arts. Denman Waldo Ross, who had studied history with Henry
Adams and art with Charles Eliot Norton, deplored the loss of pure

---

16. Impressed by the Japanese receptivity to evolution, Christopher Benfey notes, he "speculated that
Buddhism, with its cycles of extinction and reincarnation, was more compatible with Darwin than was
Christianity."

Japanese traditional art as the country turned eagerly to American and European fashions. A small Western-style portrait of him by a Japanese artist has shared a case at the MFA with two works from the Edo period (seventeenth century). Both feature kimono-ed courtesans and were part of his extensive collection.

Edward S. Morse in Yokohama

These men, all born in the early 1850s, all graduates of Harvard University, went off in their high-buttoned jackets to discover something unavailable in the Back Bay, and now I find myself wanting to follow them. For one thing, they were friends and associates of Isabella Gardner long before her friendship with Okakura. Decades before her museum took its current shape, she had opened her house in the Back Bay for Edward Morse's series of lectures on Japan, gatherings in the early 1880s that drew the attention of Brahmin society in that direction—including the young Dr. Bigelow. In 1883 the Gardners themselves traveled to the East: to Japan,

China, Vietnam, Cambodia, Java, and India. This trip was originally planned as an excursion on which Isabella would be accompanied by F. Marion Crawford, but evidence nosed out by her biographers suggests that he abruptly abandoned the relationship shortly before the trip began, and (as with the trip to Europe after the death of her child almost two decades earlier) it became the diversion that assuaged loss and opened her to wider aesthetic possibility.

A Garden Lantern

Japanese granite with tripod base in the Chinese Loggia

Much of the material pertaining to the travels remains—a window left open to a view of the past for the contemplative, and curious, future. She went with her husband, the agreeable Jack, and the papers she did not burn suggest great pleasure and interest in all she saw: wrestling matches and Buddhist temples and "pigeons whirring through the air with their strange aeolian harp music, made by the whistles in their tails!" Undaunted by the vagaries of travel, she wrote of the visit to Nikko, "It was two days there and two days back and it was hot, and one of the horses died, and the coachman got drunk, but it was all paid for by the glorious beauty of Nikko.... It is mountains, valleys, trees, waterfalls, lakes and in such a setting (with a driveway of sixty miles with a double row of grand old Cryptomerias) are the famous temples...."[17] She rode to Angkor Wat lying in a bullock cart, and camped in the jungle where the French Governor served on the 17th of November a five-course meal with four wines and Champagne. At Angkor Thom an invaluable Mr. Hunter told "wonderful

---

17. The cryptomeria allée is actually twenty-five miles long—impressive enough.

stories of capital punishments. Ten women beheaded at one time. A strange story of the King's sister and a young Siamese."

Then comes something in a slightly different tone. Returning to Penang through a palm forest she got out of the gharry and walked to a small Siamese temple, where she found "all alone...a yellow-robed priest chanting his evensong to his gilded Buddha. I crept up softly—no light but the moon and the service lamps and the burning incense, and I stood behind the priest, who never heard or noticed me. It was exquisite—but very sad."

The Road to Nikko

The sadness is key, I think: the chiaroscuro of joy and sadness, emotional pigments surprising the aesthetics, her feelings finding spiritual absorption and perhaps a different sense of her own personal loss. But this is the story I imagine; in fact I can never know what this moonlit moment meant to the often self-dramatizing Isabella. It urges me instead toward a larger story, that moment when the aesthetic and spiritual globe was expanding. The trade agreements Commodore Perry had been after brought to American drawing rooms fans, medicine boxes, ceramics, netsuke, and silk scrolls. They brought to women's fashions—first in Paris and finally in Boston—the kimono and the piled-up hairstyles of Japanese ladies. They brought images of carp and cranes, chrysanthemum and bamboo. They brought to Manet, van Gogh, Whistler, Monet, and other artists the inspiration and theory of Japanese art. For those in the right place to take notice, it was a time when cultural and commercial exchange offered the opportunity for both physical and philosophical adventure, and therefore Isabella's experience in the palm forest seems to be about something more than international trade, or even her own spiritual healing.

The Asian art connection, for all its associations with conquest and commerce, opens a different window on the story of artistic hegemony in late nineteenth-century Boston. It makes it less about putting the stamp of legitimacy on new fortunes, and more about discovering another way of imagining value altogether. It offers an aesthetic (and spiritual) escape hatch from the teleological disagreements represented by the plaster casts. It turns my search for Isabella Stewart Gardner toward the Museum of Fine Arts, and toward some others in her circle, men whose life adventures—no less than Clover Adams's or Cornelia Smith's—offer another vantage from which to see her.

"Welfare Improves with Sailing"

Inscription on a Danish silver tankard (1700) in the Dutch Room

Ernest Fenollosa, as it happens, was not a buttoned-up fellow at all. The son of a Spanish musician who had married into a prominent shipping and political family in Salem, just north of Boston, he attended that interlocking directorate of opportunity Harvard College, which is how he was brought to the attention of Morse and where he met other significant friends, including Henry Adams. Open to Japan when that opportunity knocked, and open as well to nonwestern art and the precepts of Buddhism, he was instrumental in saving much of the traditional art of Japan from being swept away by the wave of modernizing that followed the fall of the military shogunate in 1868. Even as Bostonians were wearing kimonos around the house and studying Esoteric Buddhism, Japanese ladies and gentlemen were viewing cherry blossoms and bowing to the Emperor in full Victorian regalia. In 1878 Fenollosa arrived in Tokyo to teach philosophy at the university; by 1886, as a prelude to establishing a School of Fine Arts in Japan, he was appointed (along with his former student Okakura Kakuzo) Imperial Commissioner to investigate fine art institutions in Europe and the United States. The school opened three years later, with a curriculum that linked contemporary originality to the classical past.

American Consul in Japan

On his return to Boston in 1890 he became the first curator of Asian art at the Museum of Fine Arts, and its apostle to the West. While the Japanese were being encouraged to learn and adopt Western customs and technology, and as the vogue for things oriental made Chinese and Japanese paraphernalia into a Western merchandising trope, Fenollosa had been collecting art treasures of the East and studying the art of the Noh theater. He hoped to show ordinary Americans what he saw as the superiority of ordinary Japanese aesthetic taste. By this he did not mean simply popularization of the culture, but rather the way that graceful detail was honored in even the humblest farmer's hut. He attacked the fashionable bogus Buddhism in one of F. Marion Crawford's novels as both selfish (as religion) and multicultural mishmash (as philosophy). He devoted his life to the understanding and study of Asian art and culture, even after his very successful curatorial career in Boston collapsed when he traded in his socially impeccable wife for his young assistant at the Museum of Fine Arts, Mary McNeil Scott.

Almond Trees in Spring
Watercolor by Dodge Macknight in the Macknight Room

Almost the same age as Mary Berenson, Mary McNeil Chester Scott Fenollosa was not sent to college or acquainted with important cultural figures. Yet she too had both cultural ambitions and an adventurous spirit, despite the struggles of her Alabama family after the Civil War. She married at seventeen only to be widowed while still very young. A former suitor then proposed by mail from his consular post in Japan. At twenty-five, with her little boy, she boarded a ship. "Japan was a charming dream, Scott a harsh awakening," Fenollosa's biographer Lawrence Chisolm says tersely. They had a daughter, but were divorced when his tour of duty in

Japan was over. Back in Alabama, she hoped to have a career as a writer and applied for the job at the Museum of Fine Arts as a way of getting to that great literary center, Boston.

As things turned out, the job took her back to Japan, in a position fully to penetrate its charm. Fenollosa sacrificed his Boston career in order to marry her, apparently without regret and probably to the benefit of his work.[18] If desperation had taken her to Japan as a young widow, her own ambition and confidence took her to Boston, where the relationship with Fenollosa got them both out of those narrow social confines. And if her account of his departure from the museum is discreet to the point of dissembling, it also makes very clear its benefit. "Professor Fenollosa," she writes in the introduction to his major work, "saw no future there except as a sort of showman and personal demonstrator, and as writer of sporadic catalogues." The circus of the museum, she implies, gave way to "more serious writing and lecturing," and the need to visit both European art centers and Japan. She describes him in Japan as always "studying, acquiring, reaching forward. Now it was not alone art that he pursued, but religion, sociology, the No drama, and Chinese and Japanese poetry." Their partnership, like that of the Berensons, entangled erotic and intellectual passion, the fruit of the husband's superior education eagerly shared by the wife. In the context of Eastern art and philosophy, she found her place, as Mary Berenson found hers in the world of Western art and its American collectors.

After his death she was left to bring his wide-ranging investigations of Asian culture to their fruition. Not only did she complete and publish his major work on Chinese and Japanese art, but she brought to the attention of

---

18. Although a novel he never took beyond the manuscript stage, called *His Wife's Lawyer*, does suggest a trail of inamicable feeling and financial difficulties with regard to the first Mrs. Fenollosa.

Ezra Pound his translations of early Chinese poetry, Confucian philosophy, and Noh plays. As Christopher Benfey says in his account of the Asian-American cultural moment, *The Great Wave*, this meeting between Mary Fenollosa and the experimental American poet changed the course of American literature. Her own poetry ran to charming rhymes for children,[19] but she recognized in Pound's early work the man to go through her husband's notebooks (one of which was in fact a collaboration with Okakura on a projected survey of Chinese culture), thus introducing, says Benfey, Taoism into American literature, along with "those qualities—concision, suggestivity, detachment, vivid imagery—that he found in Fenollosa's draft translations and notes." The Fenollosas made a foreign world into their home, and eventually brought it to America by their joint labors.

Ernest and Mary Fenollosa, 1900

---

19. It was the rosy flush of dawn / In beautiful Japan, / When, from the house with swinging pail, / Came little Noshi-San, / Her strapped and lacquered wooden clogs / A-clicking as she ran.

Chrysanthemums and Orchids Growing by a Rock

Applied relief on wooden doors (19c) in the second-floor
elevator passage

The Fenollosas are less well-documented but even so present a significant parallel to the Berensons: they offered the arts of the East to a culture-hungry America as the Berensons did those of Europe. Their aesthetic skills never made them wealthy, however. Fenollosa's philosophically based expertise never became directly marketable to millionaires or picture dealers, and in fact an attempt to become the American agent for a Japanese art dealer ended disastrously in lawsuits and financial loss. Mary's literary career (like F. Marion Crawford's) has vanished now, but her poetry, children's books, and novels were not a negligible contribution to this partnership. The scandal of his divorce and remarriage precluded further institutional employment for Fenollosa—and not only in Boston. Chisolm says Fenollosa was never again employed by an American museum or university. In 1901, after four years in Japan, he began his career as a lecturer on the art and culture of the Far East.

That labor was never directed toward helping people acquire the right stuff (although his experience was consulted by wealthy collectors like Charles Lang Freer). While Berenson's mission was to find a way to authenticate European masterworks—to fix history and value simultaneously—Fenollosa's mission was to change the way Westerners perceived Asian art: to show it as more than an industrial and decorative accomplishment. In classifying Chinese and Japanese art into "epochs," the point was to look at the

Orient as the aesthetic equal of the West—not only deserving the same kind of serious study, but also yielding principles that could be applied to art education in the West. He had completed only a draft manuscript when he died suddenly in London, in 1908, leaving Mary to complete *Epochs of Chinese and Japanese Art*, his major work. His ashes now lie under a grove of cryptomerias near the temple at Miidera, Japan, where he first studied Buddhism.

In 1920 a monument to his memory was erected there by his students and friends. His friend and fellow Buddhist traveler William Sturgis Bigelow added to the brief record of his life engraved there a forceful account of exactly what his services to Japan had been during the period of intense Western plunder that followed the fall of the shogunate in 1868. "Japan was swarming with foreigner merchants, who bought for a song the masterpieces of Japanese art," he says, while the impoverished Daimos, unable to provide for their retainers, "threw open their storehouses and told [them] to help themselves." Fenollosa's ability to say why one thing was better than another saved Japanese art from neglect and extinction, and brought Asian art into the realm of high culture in the West. This work was indeed a quest to bring what was foreign and invisible to a new audience. It made the project of saving a disappearing past the center of his own biography, and left the rock of his life among the flowers of the East.

A Young Commander

Painting by Justus Suttermans (17c) in the Dutch Room

The Fenollosas are a comparably influential (if less swashbuckling) contrast to the Berensons, but the contrast between Fenollosa's escape from Mrs.

Gardner's Boston and his friend Bigelow's choice not to suggests how the chill of tradition discouraged alternatives. Douglass Shand-Tucci mentions Bigelow as part of the bohemian milieu his biography weaves around Mrs. Gardner, a social world of wealthy, talented, gay and bisexual men he calls "Boston Bohemia." He was also Clover Adams's favorite cousin, although (once again) there are no letters between them left for our curious eyes. The letters of his that do remain show him as playful and self-assured; his favorite expression when declining an invitation was "my heart is a handful of dust." He studied medicine at Harvard and in Paris, but did not follow the medical profession, as his father (himself a prominent physician, and, in fact, the Gardners's family doctor) desired. With his considerable fortune he supported a well-known Wagnerian opera star, but never married her.[20]

In Japan he was not only an adherent of Esoteric Buddhism; he provided financial assistance to impoverished artists, gave $10,000 toward the establishment of the Fine Arts Academy in Japan, and made donations for the repair and conservation of temples. His own collection ran to 4,000 paintings and 50,000 prints and drawings. I think he was an idealist and an aesthete, and also a pure product of his city and class. Henry Adams described him to a friend as mistakenly seeking Paradise rather than the Fireside, although as things fell out, when his father died in 1890 he inherited a couple of firesides—two fine houses, plus an island off Nantucket—as well as trusteeships of the Museum of Fine Arts and the Massachusetts General Hospital.

---

20. "...please report me of sound & disposing mind to my father, if you see him," he wrote to Phillips Brooks in 1889. "He does not take any stock in Buddhism, & thinks that I am hovering on the verge of lunacy, because I do not come home & get up some grandchildren for him, like a well-regulated Bostonian."

Scroll Portrait of W. S. Bigelow

Granite Hawk of Horus

Egyptian sculpture (4c BC) in the Court

Home from Japan in 1889, by 1906 he had evolved (or devolved) into the trustee who resigned from the museum's board when the battle over the plaster casts was lost, and like an angry Victorian (which I suppose he now was) cut the museum out of his will. In a further move that demonstrates the unofficial network that lay behind the hereditary entitlements of Boston's cultural system, he then proceeded to try to dig up some dirt on the Museum's young director Matthew Prichard that might remove him from the museum—and perhaps also his portrait from the MacKnight Room at Fenway Court.[21]

All I'm saying is that although the teachings of Esoteric Buddhism run counter to the cultural and political hegemony such behavior implies, his

---

21. Not only did this project fail, but there is yet another portrait of Prichard in the cupboards of the Short Gallery—a sketch by Henri Matisse.

sense of himself as a player was not altered or impeded. He was a close friend of the son of that Mr. Roosevelt Clover Adams encountered on her Nile trip, the boy by this time President Roosevelt—a friendship that helped influence United States policy toward Japan and Japanese immigration. The intimacy of his access may be gauged by a letter written in 1906 from his summer place on the island, describing to the President the accommodations available in Bigelow's new house in Boston (the Fireside his father had left him turned out to be too small). The room he chooses to describe most fully is

a bathroom with sun in it, a tub big enough to float in, a 20 in tilt-up washbowl, and the harmless necessary seat so placed by the window as to command a noble panorama of Beacon St. the favorite promenade of the elite, Boston Common, the Soldiers' Monument and other points of historic interest. —By thus combining the humbler episodes of daily life with the broadest intellectual opportunities we strive to please, and to render ourselves worthy of a continuance of Official Patronage.

In the absence of a Buddhist community, he had other connections to keep him going in his later years.

Bigelow lived to the age of seventy-six, ultimately the solid granite old guard, a footnote to the story of art in Boston, despite his extensive (indispensable, really) contribution to it. Isolated from his spiritual community, but socially prominent—a divided life with excellent bathing facilities. Half his ashes are in the Mount Auburn Cemetery, which is in my neighborhood, and the other at Homyoim temple, in Japan. There are probably cryptomeria trees nearby, but like so much about him, I cannot know for sure.

The Vinegar Tasters

Two-fold screen by Kana Motonobu (17c) in the second-
floor elevator passage

If Fenollosa's story is about losing Boston and gaining Asia, Bigelow's seems to be about keeping Boston and losing Asia. What I know of his influence during his lifetime is filtered through his literary style and the art he brought to Boston. Sometimes his portrait is on display in the museum, sometimes not; embedded in circles of power, he did not need to create his own museum, nor to insist that the future share the particularity of his aesthetic pleasure.[22] In the end, his attachment to the habits of his time and place leaves him in that group of shades where flit Corinna Smith and Maud Elliott.

If I want to see the Isabella who touched Mary Berenson with her desire to love rather than to be loved, however, I must pass through the Boston-Asia story, and Bigelow's presence within it is central. In the context of Isabella's destroying so much of the evidence of who she was in private, the very evanescence of his largely unadvertised seventy-six years with the great and near-great and of the Brahmin powers he brought to preserving Asian art has put him on my wandering road. "The art of life," says Okakura, "lies in a constant readjustment to our surroundings." Bigelow was willing to taste from the foreign jars and if, like the Buddha

---

22. Not that he was philosophical about being thwarted in particular instances. A letter to his friend Cabot Lodge eight years after the matter of the plaster casts describes Isabella Gardner as "vain, meddlesome and impulsive, and I am sorry to say that I think she has not a very keen sense of the distinction between loyalty and treachery. She would make friends with anybody, or sacrifice any friend, for caprice." A couple of years on, though, they seem on good enough terms: "It was good to see you," he writes; and "Yours all atwitter," he signs an invitation to lunch. The private opinion shared with Lodge may simply show the many-layeredness of personality.

in the Sung allegory,[23] he found the vinegar bitter, the immense collection he brought to the museum also brought as curator the very person who inspired her desire to love, to find true sweetness. Attempting to transcend the divides of public/private and present/past that intend to keep me on the far side, then, I turn once more to Okakura Kakuzo.

"All Is Well at Home"

Chinese steatite seal (19c) in the Early Italian Room

With his command of both English and the classical Asian cultures, Okakura is the counterpart to these Brahmin explorers: the one who extended his hand from the East. He was Fenollosa's student, translator, and disciple in uncovering the heritage of Japanese art at a time when its aesthetic past was in serious danger from its own intense Westernizing drive. The selling off of Japan's artistic and cultural heirlooms to New World fortunes parallels the way impoverished European aristocrats were selling off their artworks, palaces, tapestries, and chapel furnishings, but in the case of Japan, and thanks to the passion of men like Fenollosa and Bigelow, those fortunes at least gave the country's art—and its philosophical underpinnings—a new home. A paradox of the plunder is that the East-West partnership embodied in Okakura's presence brought more than the objects themselves. Before Fenollosa's sweep of epochs or Pound's literary transformations, he was a breathing text. His skills and presence opened Boston's own esoteric culture as decisively as Commodore Perry opened the Japanese ports to Western trade.

Taking with me his philosophy of the tea ceremony, then, I want to look at Fenway Court with different eyes. The Buddhist meditation room

---

23. Buddhism's Sakyamuni, Taoism's Laotse, and Confucius each tasted from the jar of vinegar symbolizing life. The Buddha found it bitter, Confucius sour, Laotse sweet.

that Isabella installed after his death, with its Buddhist statues, temple banners, and folding screens, is gone now; a loophole in her will allowed the museum, short of funds in the early 1970s, to sell many of these objects and reconfigure the space. Instead, the most prominent reminder of her spiritual life is the chapel on the third floor where an Episcopal Mass is still celebrated on her birthday (no loophole in the will about that). It has over the altar a huge thirteenth-century stained-glass window from a French cathedral depicting scenes from the lives of Christian saints, something Henry Adams spotted in Paris and thought she should acquire. Yet, all our gestures, says Okakura, be they public or private, then or now, demonstrate impermanence, imperfection, and incompleteness. That chapel window, in fact, is a piece from a larger window of the cathedral at Soissons; it was removed for restorative care and somehow found its way to Paris in 1882 where it caught Adams's mousing eye.

The Chinese Room at Fenway Court

Indeed (as if to further illustrate the paradox of plunder) I imagine the chapel itself as a monument to impermanence. The French and Italian choir stalls, for example—"*genuine* Gothic woodwork" as Berenson emphasized when he was unable to beat the owner of the French ones down (his phrasing) from the asking price of 19,000 francs; "one of the rarest of curiosities" that he was having "minutely and delicately" touched up. They are certainly a genuine curiosity to discover as you ramble through the house. Their scale is somehow odd for the little room, as if they'd been put there temporarily while the cathedral was being cleaned.

From this perspective, the museum's 1935 *General Catalogue*, following what it calls "a natural itinerary, by rooms, through the building," becomes a guide as well to just such incompleteness and impermanence, to objects and paintings created for other worlds and other uses. A later version of the catalogue, *Guide to the Collection*, published in 1997, brings the material up to date, corrects mistaken attributions, and reflects current scholarship. The difference between the two is itself a guide to the impermanence of all itineraries.

Poisson d'Avril
Jointed silver fish (19c) in the Little Salon

The little song of impermanence I'm trying to sing about all this beautiful flotsam, however, is muted by Isabella's ironclad refusal to allow any changes in her arrangement of these things. It feels like resistance to Okakura's aesthetic philosophy, and suggests to me that she never quite bought his understanding of art—that "true beauty could only be discovered by one who mentally completed the incomplete." It is very difficult indeed to free oneself from self-possessiveness, and Isabella Gardner appears not to wish me to complete her. Burning her private papers, exerting control over the future of each piece in her collection, she does not want to be a character in *my* story, a piece in my experience of the beauty she has laid out for me to enjoy. She has fooled me with her apparent openness to my presence. I went to her birthday Mass on April 14, I've been touched by her dear friend's writing on the tea ceremony, but the thread I've been trying to follow is cut by the inflexibility of her arrangements.

Absent an invitation to contemplate impermanence and imperfection, to complete the fragments on display with one's own story, the dialogue at Fenway Court between old and new, decadence and vitality, acquisition and aesthetics, is in danger of feeling more like a clamorous cacophony than a sympathetic conversation. Okakura's ideas offer the possibility of painting my own chiaroscuro here, but running his ideas over her installation still feels like a wrestling match, and I like a grumpy tourist. In the face of our mutual resistance, then, in what spirit, with what spontaneity (remembering James's phrases about *his* Isabel) can these thousand trifles start to life? Who now has the power to say what's going on, to say what is the meaning of this place?

The Rape of Europa
Painting by Titian (16c) in the Titian Room

Abandoning now the biographical and historical maze, I am looking for a different sort of guide to this elusive relationship with art. Beginning again with another visit, I come into the Titian Room. Here's her great painting called *The Rape of Europa*. When she acquired it in 1896, she wrote to Berenson of two kinds of pleasure in it—her personal aesthetic joy ("an orgy of drinking myself drunk with Europa") and another joy more complicated ("she [Europa] has adorers fairly on their old knees—men of course.") An illustrated *Companion Guide* to the museum by Hilliard T. Goldfarb says that depending on the viewer's state of mind, the painting "can be a ribald or a sublime affirmation of the miracle of love." Mrs. Tharp's biography points out the putto in the painting looking up Europa's skimpy dress and also the disassembled silk Worth ball gown of Isabella's hanging beneath it. She includes as well a photograph of Isabella wearing the still-assembled dress at a rather staid-looking party. Does the installation with the former dress suggest a livelier party—the gown's former inhabitant decamped on the back of a lustful bull? Or at least that the expensive gown was also a masterpiece of seduction?

I heard one of the guards at the doorway into the Titian Room describing Isabella as having "that big mind—she knew exactly what she wanted to do." A retired art educator, he went on to explain that Titian's subject was considered very erotic in her time: the way the painter caught the moment of abduction as if it had been an irresistible shot by a morally lax photojournalist. Then he pointed out on a nearby stand the small painting of *Christ Carrying the Cross*, the work of an artist in the circle of Giovanni Bellini. She used that, he said, to calm herself down after spending time with the so stirring Titian. Is this the guard's own way of completing the artwork—perhaps finding the way Christ seems to make direct eye contact with the viewer a more important conjunction than the unfurled silk? Are the paintings together because they were purchased during the same heady period in 1896-97 (when the almost-Bellini was thought to be by Giorgione)? Or does the very quirkiness of the whole display preclude completion? The patterning around the Titian includes so many other objects—does it flow from personal associations with the dress or the pleasure of ownership, or other memories of delight comparable to that given by the painting? Is this just a tease, or is there also a tea ceremony? What is the conversation going on here, and how am I part of it?

Tale of the Genji

Pair of six-fold screens (17c) by Fujiwara Tsunenobu
in the third-floor elevator passage

Perhaps I should stop beating about the bush. What I'm really asking is, Was Isabella carrying on a conversation about sex in this room—and in her museum—a conversation about women and sex and power, as the *Boston Globe's* art critic Christine Temin once suggested? And is that a strand in my story of Isabella as well, another thread to entwine with the one strung with Corinna Smith, Mary Berenson, Bigelow, and the Fenollosas? Like Louise Hall Tharp, like Douglass Shand-Tucci, I am looking at the past with the faraway eyes of my own time and concerns. I want my road to Isabella to link up with my world, in which sex and gender are topics freely discussed, even by ladies who expect to be respected.

To that end, then, I followed Temin, who (after a short discussion of the Gardner Titian and Isabella's former ball gown) directed her readers to a bit of erotica then on display in the Museum of Fine Arts. There, in a small upstairs room within the Asian galleries, was an album of eighteenth-century Chinese erotic art that, as the curator told Temin, answers the question, "What did women in polygamous households do all day?" Naturally I didn't want to miss this. It turned out to be a series of twelve charming and delicate paintings in which refined and smiling ladies play board games, play with birds and animals, and play with each other's intimate parts in domestic surroundings as soothingly, as delightfully, well-appointed as any to be found in Boston—only Chinese, of course.

So the Chinese curiosities were back in the museum, and the conversation here (as in Lady Murasaki's eleventh-century *Tale*) was definitely about sex. On the surrounding walls were other Asian paintings whose sexual content, while not immediately apparent, was developed in the signage. An ink painting of a gnarled and eroded tree trunk by a contemporary Taiwanese artist was described as an allegory of sexual insecurity and a painful reference to the artist's recent divorce. Other educational data dealt with the place of sexual activity in Taoist philosophy. A painting by an unknown artist called *Portrait of a Lady* showed a solid and flourishing-looking old woman in a garden, surrounded by objects indicating her scholarship and knowledge of art, and her attunement to the realm of Earth and the Heavens above. These included cranes, deer, and flowers, bonsai plants, writing equipment, a landscape painting that seems like a window into a more contemplative world, and a couple of serving women preparing tea. The signage was careful to point out that she had come to this serene and well-appointed age by keeping up her sexual activity, a benefit of the Taoism implied by the presence of the deer and cranes.[24]

Maybe more important for my investigations, though, was the way these works of art were set in a kind of educational conversation with each other thanks to the act of sympathy (as Okakura puts it) with which the unseen authors of the signage, like the guard at the Gardner Museum, mentally completed them. There was something playful as well as gender-focused in the way the album of private erotic art was set among the more publicly sexual works. The museum lacks the intimacy of Fenway Court, but its very impersonality also offers the viewer a free space in which to come near the

---

24. Like the ladies in the polygamous household, she was painted in the eighteenth century, which was starting to seem like a better time for ladies than the nineteenth century, and possibly our own time as well (although the interpretation does mention that these surroundings were usually reserved for male scholar officials, so maybe not).

art. This particular intellectual play with the charming and polymorphous Chinese curiosity, moreover, was not part of an interpretive arrangement set in perpetuity. Impermanent as an unfurled tea leaf, all the ladies and all the signage (and the Taiwanese divorce tree as well) were gone the next time I visited the room—the display now devoted to natural objects for scholarly contemplation. In my own conversation, however, this portrait of a lady surrounded by the symbols of her power remained resonant.

Chinese Portrait of a Lady

Portrait(s) of a Lady

Sargent painting in the Gothic Room; Sargent watercolor
in the Macknight Room

The title of the Taoist portrait evokes, of course, not only Henry James's Isabel Archer—her failed quest to be as much at the center of life as the fortunate Chinese lady—but also the famous portrait of Isabella Stewart Gardner by John Singer Sargent. There are actually two portraits by Sargent in the Gardner Museum, the second and smaller one done less than two years before her death, both showing Isabella at the center of at least her own life, if not all of Earth and Heaven. In both her figure is very much the whole story, with no cranes or peonies or other coded philosophical commentary.

J. S. Sargent,
Isabella Stewart Gardner

In the one known as *Portrait of a Lady* she is standing directly facing the viewer wearing a long dark dress with short sleeves and a heart-shaped neckline, the point of the heart just low enough to show a bit of cleavage. Behind her is a series of golden circular patterns, like a mandala or the background of a thirteenth-century religious painting. The way the design works, she appears to have both a crown on her head and a halo around it. (So maybe there is some coded iconography, but it seems to have more to do with flattery than information.) It's different from other portraits of Sargent's rich clients, which generally emphasize flowing hair and silks, turning even children's mysterious faces into a performance of wealth and ease. In this one the performance assumes the viewer's direct engagement: the lady looks straight out from above the heart-shape, and the black velvet dress is merely background for her bare arms and the doubled rope of pearls circling her famous waist. (Morris Carter's biography says the portrait took nine tries to complete—to Sargent's despair—but that she was enjoying it.)

The theatricality of this image is matched in the later portrait, a small watercolor in which the sitter is swathed in white fabric from head to foot, sitting on a divan, a pillow supporting her back. This one is called *Mrs. Gardner in White*, and has a slightly exotic feel to it. She is covered except for her face, but it's as if the face is only momentarily exposed, as if she were an Arab woman or a figure from antiquity. There's no hint that by this time she had been partially disabled by a stroke, and was in fact propped on the pillow. On the other hand, the portrait does seem to show a face being absorbed by surroundings that are themselves thinning out. Where in the earlier portrait her flesh came forward from deep gold-red and vivid black, here the red is a few streaks on the pillows, the gold a muted yellow barely sketched on the slipcover. The shadows on her robes shade into deeper shadow behind her. The face is ageless, but it's clearly a function of the painter's tact, not the lady's religious practices. By this time she was in her eighties, and for Sargent a lady's face was not the place to demonstrate his mastery of realist technique.

Perhaps more to the point, unlike the Taoist Lady in the garden of her achievements, she is still alone, still the whole story. Only when considered side by side might these two portraits invite meditation on the impermanence of personality. But these paintings are not side by side, nor is there any signage to indicate how they fit with other objects in their rooms. In the case of the earlier one, it's not hard to discover that in its time it created a stir for its sexual content. Possibly the bit of cleavage was not balanced by enough attention to the costliness of the dress, or maybe the arms frame the flexible silk purse of the waist too boldly. The gossip that wafts across the century includes a joke about Sargent having "painted her all the way down to Crawford's Notch," a sample of Boston men's club wit that puns on a well-known resort in the White Mountains and her relationship to F. Marion Crawford. Sexual activity at the time not being part of religious observance, this painting (like the ones in the Chinese album) was kept at home for private enjoyment. Even today it doesn't greet the visitor anywhere near the entrance to the Gardner Museum. To see it you have to climb all the way up to the third floor, where it's displayed in a corner of the criminally badly lit Gothic Room.

The later portrait is about as far away from this as the museum allows. Sargent's watercolor is in the Macknight Room, on the first floor, near the front door. This is the room where Morris Carter lived when he was finally allowed to bring in his trunks. Matthew Prichard lived here while he was acting director of the Museum of Fine Arts. Sargent lived in it while he was painting the portrait upstairs. As it can be easily closed off when the museum is short of guards, often it's not even open, so it retains an impression of being a sort of inner sanctum. You enter through a double set of doors, the inner one with a portrait on it of Macknight himself. Dodge Macknight was a painter whose work she liked, bought, and hung—enough of it to give the room its name. In spite of its four tall windows the room seems small and intimate. And in spite of its sparse furnishings, rather crowded.

Hand-Mirror (with handle made from knitting-needle case)

Dutch mirror (19c) in the Macknight Room

When Sargent had finished this portrait Isabella propped it on a bookcase where she could see it from her seat in front of the fire. There it remains, one among many objects on the bookcase (including another portrait by Sargent, in charcoal, of the handsome archeologist Thomas Whittemore in a sort of fez). Standing before it you have to tilt your neck up, and stand on one side to avoid the reflection from the glass covering it.

J. S. Sargent,
Mrs. Gardner in White

As I am studying the aged Isabella sitting against her pillows staring into the future that will not be hers (despite her efforts here), the guard comes over to intensify my experience. "That's Mrs. Gardner," he tells me in a deep Russian accent, "and she was painted right here in this room." In fact, he goes on, she was sitting right there, on that couch. He points to a low settee with a caned seat under an opposite window. It is clearly not the comfy, pillow-strewn couch in the painting. My doubtful noises spur him to discover internal documentation — the bit of frame behind her, which he says is the window, but now looks to me like part of another painting (an observation I keep to myself).[25] Warming to his theme, he makes a perpendicular gesture toward the window behind the settee. "So," he informs me in Slavic basso, "you have the opportunity to touch history."

That is, of course, what I am trying to do, and I put up no further resistance to his misinformation. As the uncontrollable future, we are completing the incomplete, and I am now looking for the portrait of Matthew Prichard. I want to see the face Bigelow hated and I find it, after some trouble, on a desk covered with the usual thousand trifles: a hand mirror made from a knitting-needle case, candlesticks, Japanese cigarette boxes, letter openers, bottles, etc. Prichard is in profile, with a sharp nose, a youthful seriousness. In his high collar and smoothly brushed back hair, it's hard to imagine him as a man who would infuriate the old guard, or ever be "down on his luck" (as Mrs. Tharp says he was after he left the museum).

Who was he, and who was the Isabella Gardner he knew? What came between the black-velvet-and-pearls and the white drapery? How does this small crowded room help me mentally to complete the portrait? My brief

---

25. Later another guard suggested that the vague image behind her is perhaps a reflection in a mirror. Then she pointed out in the dim light the shape of a slightly demonic face looking over Isabella's left shoulder, "like an animus."

hermeneutic struggle with the Russian guard returns me to the biographical and historical junk piled off-canvas—to the evidence she systematically destroyed in the fireplace across the room. Did she indeed learn from Okakura to care less about the razzle-dazzle of inspiring devotion and more about the sweeter private search to give love? I am trying to see her secrets— what is not on display. I want to know what she burned, to go beyond the letters and journal entries about her travels—the colorful silks and curious customs, the heat and rain and those amazing miles of cryptomeria trees and Hong Kong harbor at sunset, naked wrestlers and the eating of her first peacock, the Chinese shopkeepers of Saigon who twang their guitars all night long "or do some banging, clanging, firecrackery thing to frighten away the evil spirits." Abruptly abandoned by Frank Crawford, she was royally entertained not long afterwards by colonial administrators, and received in her diamonds by the local royalty. (Unlike Clover Adams, she didn't have to cook up transcultural ruses to prevent Jack and herself from being served meals of garlic and waste messes.) The annotations in her album of souvenir photographs are written in a firm and generous hand: "We left Nara at 1 p.m."

Matthew Prichard

It's all very entertaining, but in fact I am not touching history. I have no idea what Isabella really made of the East. The trip moved westward to India, the Middle East, and eventually came to rest in Venice. About the state of her heart we have no information at all. She did not see Frank Crawford again for ten years.

Mrs. Gardner's Japanese Travel Journal

I am looking for the story that can explain to me better her powers, her palazzo, and her talent for her own life. In my story, then, I am giving her what Jane Austen calls *elasticity of mind*: "that disposition to be comforted, that power of turning readily from evil to good, and of finding employment which carried her out of herself, which was from nature alone. It was the choicest gift of Heaven. . . ." This could be what made Isabella so appealing to so many. Even after painful disappointment she was open to the life around her. That, too, is necessary for love. Perhaps it is what the Taoists mean by attunement to the realm of Earth and Heaven above, what Okakura means by constant readjustment to our surroundings. I may just be making this up because I am glad to remember Austen's phrase and because after all this writing about Isabella I am wanting to like her, to feel that *facilité à vivre*, to bring her closer to me. And my question about the sexual conversation has not been answered. I am trying to complete her, to let the details emerge, to linger in her beautiful foolishness.

Landscape with Obelisk

Painting on wood by Govaert Flinck (17c) in the Dutch Room (stolen)
[until 1984 this painting was attributed to Rembrandt]

To this end I finally spent some time with her friend Crawford, reading a couple of novels, and even a biography of him as well. He occupies a corner of literary history that ought to have its own Library of Congress catalog category: Successful Writers Once Taken Seriously Who Are Now Dead as the Dodo. Francis Marion Crawford, Frank to his intimates, was fourteen years younger than Isabella. Maud Howe Elliott says, "Nothing he ever wrote compared with his brilliant talk," which I think she meant as a compliment but also suggests the way even a vibrant person can simply disappear, no matter how many volumes he leaves behind. His novels represent a kind of fiction he passionately believed in, one that is still recognizable in Hollywood today: "rapidly moving narrative and dramatization of ideal conduct against a backdrop of realistic settings . . . the story was the thing; the great requirement motion," as his biographer John Pilkington describes it. He wrote thirty-two novels to wild literary and popular acclaim.

His success disgusted Henry James: "What you tell me of the success of [Crawford's] last novel sickens and almost paralyses me," he wrote to a friend after the publication of a novel called *A Roman Singer* in 1884.

> It seems to me (the book) so contemptibly bad and ignoble that the
> idea of people reading it in such numbers makes one return upon

one's self and ask what is the use of trying to write anything decent or serious for a public so absolutely idiotic.... Work so shamelessly bad seems to me to dishonour the novelist's art to a degree that is absolutely not to be forgiven; just as its success dishonours the people for whom one supposes one's self to write.

James was a decade older than Crawford; by this time he had written *The Portrait of a Lady* and a good deal more. His designs on the shape of fiction's future were entirely different from Crawford's, and as things have turned out no one would mistake him for a dodo (and even the movies are willing to take a stab at his material). Nevertheless, one does sympathize with his position, particularly after spending some time with Crawford. By now shamelessness and dishonor seem less to the point than the way the motion and skill in these novels are dissipated on conventions concerning

Francis Marion Crawford

human motivation as airless and hidebound as Bigelow's insistence on the traditional status of the plaster casts.

The one called *To Leeward*, written in 1883, right after the break with Isabella Gardner, worries the problem of a woman whose love for her husband is insufficient, and her relationship with an irresistible, courtly, tender, and vital lover. Whether this describes a Gardner-Crawford triangle, nineteenth-century letter-and-journal fires conceal from us, but it is nonetheless a reasonable plot for the practice of a novelist's art.[26] Unlike James, however, who can twist social behavior, psychology, and feeling into the finest pashmina threads, Crawford can't give up an admiration for manners, courtesy, grace, and perfect deportment that feels like itchy wool against the skin.

To make a long story short, in the process of trying to kill her lover the betrayed husband kills his wife—yet lives on "well-known in Rome for his honesty, his honour, and his unaffected good sense" (no mention of legal intervention). The lover, his wonderful qualities intact, does not die. The wife pays for the whole thing, and the world is well rid of her, what with her philosophical leanings and an unappealing general dissatisfaction with life that she "found means to alleviate...in the small luxuries and amenities of life." She is a woman "strong and radiantly human" whose studies are a refuge from the improbability of being loved "by some one manly man, and loved with all the strength he had overwhelmingly." Her desire veers between material beauty and "a half-religious, half-poetic melancholy." You can see how this kind of thing would make James want to claw his skin off. The character may or may not be a cruel comment on Isabella Gardner's spiritual and material passions, but either way the

---

26. In fact, Crawford himself later regretted publishing the novel, with its severe judgment on social transgression and the possibly hurtful message to Mrs. Gardner.

dramatization is definitely not nudging the novelist's art in the direction of the twentieth century.[27]

NO8DO

(No Me Ha Dejado)
("She Has Not Abandoned Me") Spanish tile in the Spanish Cloister

In the absence of her own testimony, faced with James's visceral literary opinion and Crawford's ossified novelizing, my efforts to imagine this possibly foolhardy friendship are somewhat short-circuited by the suggestion that a woman who studies up on her philosophical interests is simply sublimating romantic disappointment (I mean, they did read Dante together). Was Crawford in fact a foolish choice for Isabella's affections?

Or was there more to it than a manly man's romance? When I read about Corinna Smith's solitary pursuit of Arabic, of Mary Berenson's unacknowledged erudition, or Clover Adams's draping her knowledge of Greek in Worth gowns, it makes me think that Isabella Gardner's attraction to beautifully educated young men may have served a purpose perhaps not as obvious as the gossip columns suggested. To enjoy the wider world women needed links to men who were conversant with it. Frank Crawford was a cultural phenomenon of the time—quite learned, in fact. He read Latin and Greek, studied Sanskrit, kept up his Urdu by keeping a diary in that language, and was fluent in Italian, French, German, and Spanish. He thought of himself as a serious historian and his lectures on Italian and Vatican history were well attended.

---

27. His biographer suggests that Mrs. Gardner's first attraction for Crawford was the luxury of her surroundings. "She lived" he says, "as he wished to live." Their friendship developed quickly; however, in a fragment of a letter Isabella cut up but did not burn, Crawford told her he thought of his first novel, *Mr. Isaacs*, as "someone else's work, as indeed it is, love, for without you I should never have written it."

If one is not disturbed by gossip (or indeed thrives on it) the pointedly erotic potential of such a youthful male entourage makes a nice cover for whatever education it offered. And if the extramarital conversation with one of these young men, perhaps fatally conventional, fired her erotic imagination, the eventual obsolescence of his work did not contaminate hers.[28] The loss of Crawford, like the loss of her loved baby son almost two decades before, in fact led her to new artistic worlds. Elasticity makes much possible, even if the actual processes through which the healing was accomplished are hidden behind a tapestry of gossip. She was not a Taoist like the lady in the eighteenth-century Chinese portrait, but into age she continued to attract and keep around her well-educated and artistically adventurous young men. Sargent, Prichard, the Berensons, Joe-rinna Smith, Okakura, and Morris Carter...she seems well beyond Crawford's crabbed imagination. (And after he was gone she joined—was *invited* to join—Professor Norton's Dante Circle.)

It's impossible to say if the stylish eccentricity so useful to a woman in claiming social authority in the late nineteenth century worked as well in a learning mode, or how entwined was Isabella's interest in art and music and literature with her pleasure in the company of artistic young men. Whatever the personal lapses, evasions, mistakes, sorrows, or embarrassments she put to the fire before she died, her openness to new possibility and to the future has meant that what she did leave to us is still alive. Whether she and Crawford disagreed about chastity or plaster casts is simply unknowable. What is clear is that the flexible silk purse of her mind has turned out to be more generous than the tireless industry of his. Perhaps to endure, to be able

---

28. Crawford seems to have had his own half-religious, half-poetic melancholy. Check out the sonnet he wrote her in 1882, for example, which begins, "My lady late within my chamber tarried" and ends, "The heart's sweet soil is not so scant or shallow/But it may feed a rose—or hold a cross"—a tidbit of sexual and religious jumble that somehow escaped the fire.

to remain meaningful as time elapses and death eats everyday life, requires the kind of flexibility and *facilité* that Isabella Gardner brought to her relationships and to her great project.

Part Three

Trumpeters, and Ladies
Conversing with a Gentleman
Tapestry fragments (16c) in the Tapestry Room

Here I am defending her now, even as I am looking for my own elasticity, the spot where the barrier between us can soften. Even as I speculate about Isabella's world, that lost place with its interesting erotic and educational issues, it still seems impervious to my play with history, or my judgment. Her relationship to Crawford represents my distance: no one back there wanted me to know what it was, and I am just running my personality over the fragments of the story. The conventions of privacy, which James was able to manipulate into modernism, keep Crawford's art trivial, leaving little for the belated reader to contemplate or complete. His best-selling page-turners might as well be in Urdu for all the power they have to draw me close to his appeal for Isabella, or to slip through the nets of time. To touch her I will need another guide, a different friend. Again I think of that younger friend of her later life, Okakura Kakuzo, who is congenial to us both.

Once more I pick up the broken thread of the tea ceremony; Okakura still represents to me, as he may have to her, a bridge into another world. He came to work with the Brahmin patriarchy at the Museum of Fine Arts, and he observed the capitalist sport of private art collection. The Americans he encountered were simultaneously inheritors of the Railway Gallop and enormous fortunes. "Limitless indeed," he observes in *The Book of Tea*, "must be the capacity for artistic feeling in those who can exist day after day in the midst of such confusion of colour and form as is to be often seen in the homes of Europe and America." His irony tickles the edges of politeness, and finally describes a persistent Western dilemma. In a democratic age, as he says, everyone wants what is supposed to be the best, without consulting their own

97

feelings: "They want the costly, not the refined; the fashionable, not the beautiful." How indeed are Americans to reach the beauty in objects they have acquired from cultures not their own?

Perhaps in the interest of friendship, Okakura simply dissolved the discontinuities of Mrs. Gardner's personality and collecting in a "crystal night" of poetry. His stairway of jade refines and transforms her eclectic collection, her fragmentary conversation, into one lovely (if imperial) object. But mostly Fenway Court is open during the day, and in the room with the great Titian painting alone the *General Catalogue* lists almost one hundred other objects: bottles, vases, hangings, busts, tables, chests, chairs, and that studio Tintoretto painting over the doorway that is very difficult to see at all. The daylight experience of this willful installation of her famous *plaisir* invites the visitor in many directions at once; it is very difficult to come to friendship—to be assaulted by the contradictions Okakura describes and still let the smallest details emerge into sight.

"Cognoies Toy Mesme"
("Know Yourself") motto on set of Worcester armorial china (18c)
in the Yellow Room

In search of an aesthetic *facilité* that will allow me to knot together Fenway Court and Okakura's *Book of Tea*, I discovered a contemporary dive into the tea aesthetic, *Wabi-Sabi for Artists, Designers, Poets & Philosophers*, by Leonard Koren. Brief and illuminating, Koren is in conversation with Okakura, opening the teahouse again, offering a way to reencounter the things we have been left from the past. Wabi-sabi (and by extension the tea aesthetic), as he explains it, is about what we can hardly see when we look at things: "this faint evidence [the things of our lives, he means], at the borders of nothingness." Like ourselves, things are always evolving from or devolving into nothingness; thus "nothingness itself—instead of being empty space, as in the West—is alive with possibility." Reaching back through Koren, I am imagining the nothingness of Isabella, her absence, alive at the borders, the past visible at the borders of the present. And this sense of evanescent possibility around things, this moment of grace, doesn't have to be sought in a lowly Japanese farmer's hut, or even in a perfectly proportioned eighth-century Japanese temple. Why not in a massive stone museum fifty miles from Plymouth Rock—a temple called into being by wealthy industrialists—or a mock-Venetian palazzo on the Fenway nearby? Even if the Buddha Room at the Museum of Fine Arts is a bit of a theme space, and at Fenway Court the historical past feels like a foreign culture to be sorted out, the art still offers a way to be with it and to come closer to its inhabitants. This was Fenollosa's path through the seeming aporias of time and space, and his student Okakura's as well.

Memoriae

Three manuscripts from books of hours (15c) in the Long Gallery

Just outside the Buddha Room, then, is a well-lit hall with glass display cases for smaller objects, like Edward Sylvester Morse's set of Japanese tea caddies, forty-four little brown stoneware pots. In a nearby room are a Tang horse bending its neck to bite its knee, and a Sui era swoop-necked Bactrian camel with Persian and Indian musical instruments hanging from its humps. These things, simultaneously forceful evocations of other worlds and faint evidence (in Koren's phrase) of something forever lost, are simply suspended in the vacuum of their acquisition.

In his chapter on Taoism, Okakura discusses Laotse's metaphor of the vacuum—that reality is found in the vacant space of a room, not the walls and roof that enclose it. A pitcher's usefulness is in the emptiness that may be filled, not in its shape or material. "In vacuum alone motion is possible," he says. In art, this means leaving something unsaid so that the beholder may complete the idea: "A vacuum is there for you to enter and fill up to the full measure of your aesthetic emotion."

Those little brown tea caddies, then: you can read the modest signage about Morse and about what they're made of, fall under the spell of their modest shapes, think about the jumble of your own modest tea equipment. The world they came into is gone, and so is the world in which Morse gave them to the museum. Yet the borders of nothingness are infinitely permeable to the mind's slightest touch. The Sui camel, with its snooty camel stare, the hatlike mane behind its ears, its extra-long legs, its miraculous earthenware longevity, and the little water jars on either side of the back hump, *and dimly in the background a jumble of camel drivers and tourists gesture against an Egyptian morning sky*, is here and not here. I am simultaneously in this moment and elsewhere; briefly part of the surprising ivory-colored U-shaped camel neck, and touching its long past with my short one.

At the same time a docent is showing a group of high school students the dripped glazes on the Tang horse, helping them to see the perfect imperfection. Education and pleasure and past and present collapse. What are these things doing in this place? And why are we here with them, now? What would Okakura say of this display today?

Maybe that they are there as they have always been, at the edges of nothingness, and that the lessons of the tearoom (all things are impermanent, all things are imperfect, all things are incomplete) are not incompatible with the loosely structured rituals of museum strolling. In the Buddha Room, arranged behind glass, or fastened in place by the will of a woman long dead, the surprise of what is beautiful emerges from the murk and confusion of convention.

A She-Goat

Painting by Rosa Bonheur in the Blue Room

This wabi-sabi is almost an anti-aesthetic; it notices the tentative and ephemeral, "the exact opposite of the Western ideal of beauty as something monumental, spectacular, and enduring," Koren says. Yet Isabella Gardner's will specified that nothing in Fenway Court was to be changed, removed, rethought. Okakura's poem may have dissolved Fenway Court in moonlight, but *"C'est Mon Plaisir"* is still cast in stone above the entrance. She intended to fix that pleasure with her will, still crying out in the voice of her old age, "Don't touch!" Her plans for the museum fit within a tradition of completion and endurance, and the contradiction between the free-playing pleasure she took in creating it and the constraints she placed on the longevity she imagined for it is perplexing. To Berenson she wrote, "The Abode of Shadow—(this is what *Fenway* means in Japanese)," and included with her letter a copy of Okakura's poem. Nevertheless, her spectacular and enduring creation is officially complete, and does not seem to linger at the borders of nothingness or shadow. Perhaps that is why it is so hard to find her in her Abode. The act of sympathy, the sympathy that arises from noticing the nothingness we share—and its possibilities—is blocked by the imperious self-possession with which she marked Fenway Court. Her shadow, thrown across the years, obscures my relations with it. Perhaps I am trying too hard— I don't want to be stretching my elasticity to the breaking point.

As it happens, though, as it always happens, there is more to the story.

Isabella herself may or may not have been changed by what she felt standing by the little Siamese temple in the moonlight, or by Okakura's lessons on seeking love, but the history of the museum itself bears out some of the deeper principles of the tea ceremony. Even her will is necessarily a work of incompleteness and imperfection, and so Fenway Court has opened to the shadowy Future, which has its own paradoxes of preservation and plunder. The scattering of her meditation room[29] does feel like a loss, and yet it seems as metaphorically appropriate to a philosophy of wabi-sabi as the preserved curiosities of the chapel are to the Western longing—with its paradoxes of preservation and plunder—to overcome death. Later losses point even more dramatically to the importance of honoring ephemerality. Devolution and evolution find their place in even the most exacting specifications about the future; they make room for absence, and for new ideas, and for perplexity like my own about my presence in Isabella's aesthetic world.

Scenes from the Metamorphoses of Ovid
Paintings over the door (16c) in the Short Gallery

Sometimes when you are cruising the cases in a museum there will be an empty space with a little card indicating that some piece of porcelain or bronze or jade, some bowl or amphora, or a painting has been removed. It's a gap in the display, a little jolt in the experience. A reminder that you are not in eternity here, but in a workplace. Even here there is process, change, absence. In French these little cards are known as *fantômes*, phantoms, ghosts. They are, however, very literal ghosts — reassurances that

---

29. As noted earlier, its subterranean location on the south side of the building exempted it from the general constraints of her will.

the missing item will be returned. For over a decade now at the Gardner Museum there have been no *fantômes* for a dozen absent pieces; instead there are small signs that report a theft. On March 18, 1990, two thieves dressed as Boston policemen entered the building and removed some of the art. None of it has ever been traced.

In improvised compliance with the directives of Isabella's will, beneath the painting of Manet's mother in the Blue Room there remained for many years the empty hooks from which hung his small oil portrait called *Chez Tortoni*. In the Dutch Room the frames from which the paintings were cut still remain on the wall in their designated positions. Instead of *A Lady and Gentleman in Black* and *Storm on the Sea of Galilee*, both by Rembrandt, frames now enclose only sections of the green brocade-covered walls where the paintings once hung. *The Concert* by Vermeer and *The Obelisk* by Govaert Flinck were once propped back to back with a piece of seventeenth-century Italian velvet draped between them; now you see only brown velvet through their frames. The room still has plenty of other stuff, including a Dürer portrait, a Rembrandt self-portrait, a couple of Holbeins, a Van Dyck—and that's not even to mention the collectibles, which include a French provincial bread cooler, a German silver ostrich, a Han earthenware dog, and a small Chinese pig carved out of serpentine and possibly used as a token of greeting to the spirit world.[30] Even so, the absent works have a dominating presence. Like Isabella herself, they now invite extra-aesthetic speculation. They are a scandal, a sign of impermanence, a loss, an absent presence.

The unmoved frames bring into focus how forcefully her willful pleasure and presence remain in the high-ceilinged rooms, in the glass-

---

30. In fact this wonderful little pig is positioned right in front of one of the emptied frames, where it's possibly in touch with the painting's spirit right now.

covered courtyard and the loggias around it. And still she is so difficult to meet. Biographers have tangled—scrupulously, curiously, enthusiastically—with her pleasure and her will. Sargent idealized her in two different ways. Anders Zorn painted her in dynamic motion in Venice in 1894; James McNeill Whistler drew her as *A Little Note in Yellow and Gold*—a small pastel experiment on cardboard.[31] In 1917 Martin Mower offered her seriously hatted and reading through a spotted veil. Her palazzo on the Fenway, however, that Renaissance-inspired autobiography, taunts me like an empty frame. It does not willingly show me Okakura's friend.

A View Across a River

Painting by Gustave Courbet in the Blue Room

Vacuum, replies Okakura, is art's first medium. And art is always in motion, finding new places for itself. Nothingness is alive with possibility, and along with the rest of us, young artists are drawn to the Gardner Museum. The year after the theft the French artist Sophie Calle created *fantômes* for the stolen works by interviewing those who had been closest to them. She asked curators, guards, and other staff members to talk about the missing paintings, and used their words to create descriptive collage texts that she framed like paintings. Thus memory, language, and reading substitute for the lost objects and the encounter with them. Calle is a photographer, and she also photographed the stripped spaces, the former abodes of the stolen works. These images she put in frames that match the ones around the memory texts, and hung them in pairs, side by side. The series is called *Last Seen . . .* ;

---

31. In the summer of 1890 Henry Adams noted in a letter that James M. Whistler was painting her portrait. "Think of being the victim of Whistler," he wrote, "after being clubbed by Sargent!"

it's a crime story and it's wabi-sabi; it's a conjunction of sensational loss, emptiness, and possibility. The thieves created a vacuum within Isabella Gardner's permanent arrangements; Calle entered it with *her* pleasure and *her* will. The lost paintings have become what she's made of their memory, and her viewers now complete the masterpiece. Image has turned into text; text itself has become the image. Devolution and evolution seem simultaneous here.

Sophie Calle, *Last Seen . . .*
(*Storm on the Sea of Galilee*)

In one of the paintings taken from the Dutch Room Rembrandt's Biblical storm is (still, I hope; somewhere) a large, dramatically lit sea scene: huge sky and waves, boat tipped forward toward the viewer, fourteen men dealing with the elements. Christ, just awakened, is dealing with it by rebuking his disciples for their lack of faith. The fourteenth member of the party is Rembrandt himself, the only one with his attention turned away from either Christ or the boat. He's looking out of the painting, back at the viewer, an image of Okakura's point about art, the "secret understanding between the masters and ourselves," the way we are taken into their confidence. The text-comments in Calle's *fantôme* express that understanding in various ways. One viewer was upset by Rembrandt's presence—it seemed arrogant. Another found it humble that the painter was willing to participate in this scary event.[32] Another said for sure this was where Hitchcock got the idea for his cameo appearances in his movies (adding that Rembrandt was the best-looking man in the boat and they used to call him Robert Redford). Still another pointed out that he was in fact facing "across the centuries" the large Rembrandt self-portrait hanging on the opposite wall of the room, an earlier work.[33]

One remembered that it was a very bad storm, and someone was throwing up; someone else the small delicate brushstrokes that made the foam on the waves. "Everyone is working to save His neck and He's the only one that isn't working at all," said one of them about Christ, adding, "That's how you know He's God." Another didn't remember Jesus at all in the painting, but instead a luscious seascape, a contagious chaos: "It just felt like your adrenaline picked up when you looked at the picture." And the last one remembers a five-pound box of candy received as a child from a dear family friend that had a reproduction of this painting on the lid: "It was my prized possession. I loved it, absolutely loved it." There are fourteen speakers in this text-boat, themselves now the fourteen passengers. Instead of Rembrandt's dramatic lighting, Calle offers the stereoscopic tension between the text and the large photograph of the paintingless green brocade wall, a broken fragment of Mrs. Gardner's massive installation.

---

32. Possibly suggesting that the Bible, too, waits for readers to complete it.

33. Note the temporal collapse between Rembrandt and the (in fact centuries-later) viewer.

A Small Chinese Pig

Serpentine tomb figure (3c BC) in the Dutch Room

The Vermeer phantom implies a different experience. The painting is much smaller, and had been displayed in a way that made it difficult for more than one person at a time to see it. Isabella bought it at auction in Paris in 1892. (She paid 29,000 francs—more than Berenson's choir stalls eight years later, but still only about $6,000.) She was entirely following her own taste—Berenson was not yet advising her, and Vermeer was not a chic choice. A century later, in Boston, one of her workers told Calle the painting suggested a space too private to intrude upon, another reported simply coming to see it in private, before the day began or at night after the museum was closed. Just so do viewers enter Vermeer's distant world, as I am trying to enter Isabella's.

When I first read this composite text, in a show at the Museum of Modern Art in New York, I thought it was by Calle herself, recreating the lost painting in words. Line by line, though, it seemed schizophrenic: one describes the sexual message of the painting Vermeer has reproduced on the back wall of his music room, the next the way the light and color work, then the heavy oriental rug over a piano[34] in the foreground, or the black-and-white floor tiles. "The beautiful thing about this Vermeer is that you have silence in a concert. You are looking at such stillness and yet you know they're making music," is followed by, "I didn't like it much, not my style." Now I see that Calle's assemblage reveals the multiplicity of sympathy in art; it can hold and speak back to so many separate consciousnesses.

There's more to it than that, though. An artist born long after Isabella

---

34. A mis-memory; the rug is draped over a table. The piano had yet to be invented when Vermeer painted the picture, but the imperfection of the viewer is tugging the work into his own world.

was dead is opportunistically using the way part of her distant world has been stolen, her will criminally violated, to make a resonant present. Calle doesn't need biographical material or theoretical philosophical explanations. She has gone directly to what is in fact missing and appropriated the empty space. She has incorporated Isabella Gardner's past, her fixed abode, into a meditation on how art works now. She lets go of Mrs. Gardner and her autocratic creation—the ways in which, like Crawford's novels, it doesn't transcend its own time—without losing the pleasure and presence of what she did leave us. Isabella's frustrating privacy becomes instead like the privacy in Vermeer's painting: she is now lit by the light of another world. She vanishes into the past, leaving us to share with her what she has left, however we like. As we do with James's novels, and as we take from history what is useful for the present.

As her travels brought Isabella recovery from her personal losses (and some great paintings to Boston), Calle's elastic art practices have recovered a new life for the lost paintings. Isabella Gardner's desire to fix the conditions under which our education and enjoyment should take place has been undermined by the passage of time, but *Last Seen...* suggests a happy conjunction between two different beauties—Western art and wabi-sabi—that was unable to happen in Mrs. Gardner's Boston. It frames the necessary sympathetic completion by the viewers, even as its very possibility is premised on the loss of the artworks themselves. Like the little Chinese pig, her many-voiced phantom greets the spirit world, the absent presence of the paintings.

The Spirit of the Water Lily

Watercolor study by John La Farge in the Blue Room

Now I am willing to try again, to stand myself at the borders of her absence, to approach Isabella's world in a spirit of wabi-sabi, to let her imperious will dissolve like Meiji Japan, like Bigelow's Boston, into the art that has crossed the border of time. In the Macknight Room there's a painting of a cascade of nasturtiums spilling from a window down the wall of the courtyard just outside. That particular scarlet sight—like the annual Mass on Isabella's birthday—is recreated every year. When I step into the courtyard, brilliant with spring light under the immense paned roof, the nasturtiums are falling in tangled color from the window railings. Beyond the curved glass above, clouds are moving swiftly; water splashes gently from two stone dolphins into the pool beneath the double staircase; massed pots of blue hydrangeas intensify the light. Visitors perch at the edges of the courtyard, staring upwards at the pink walls and the open windows into the galleries. At the borders of my mind there's a brief buzzing about simulacra (is this just a Disneyland of bygone wealth?) and then it quiets.

Walking through the galleries on the upper floors you are constantly pulled toward this courtyard light, and yet there is so much to stop for and love in the old and beautiful paintings—in spite of the awkwardness often required to actually see them. One of my favorites is a Pollaiuolo portrait of a Florentine woman in profile. There's something terrifically unideal about her, the shadowed curves of her face, her oddly wrapped hair, and the completely unlikely way her breasts fit into the green bodice of the dress. Across the room Raphael's portrait of Tommaso Inghirami shows a massive red-draped figure with a book open in front of him. Also an ink bottle and paper, on which he seems to be writing while also keeping his eye on God, or maybe just the Pope (could have been either: he was a Vatican secretary and also a witty playwright). It's hung in a corner by a window, and you can't quite get in front of it because of a desk whereon is propped a smaller Raphael, a bit from the predella of an altarpiece, a Lamentation, a Pieta, that you sort of crouch down to see. Does it matter to me what Isabella was thinking when she put this arrangement together?

The Courtyard

In the Gothic Room upstairs I finally ask the guard. Why are all those little portraits in the frieze high up under the ceiling so badly lit that you can hardly see them at all? At first he says he doesn't know, but then it turns out he does. He suggests that they are actually not such great art, that the fifteenth-century Italians who commissioned them were just looking for a way to decorate. He points out that many of them repeat, that they were the kind of thing turned out by the yard. I am delighted—they are supposed to be like a wallpaper border; the dimness of the room is not necessarily meant to frustrate. He thinks, though, that they were not bought all at once, but collected and then put up as a frieze. The presence of art, of the past, hovers in the hall-like space above the wheeled stone window, the Venetian fireplace, the leather and wooden furniture, the Simone Martini *Madonna and Child*, and, most astonishing, the Giotto panel propped on an easel by the Venetian windows at the end of the room. This small treasure from the fourteenth century was part of an altarpiece now scattered in parts to Munich, New York, Florence, London.

Oh, Isabella, how excited you were to get this, how persuasive Berenson's description: "Then look how delicately intimate is the movement of the Child toward the extended hands of His mother," he wrote to her, as if she were beside him, admiring. "There are any number of maws gaped wide to swallow it," he added, urging her not to lose the chance to snag it. Now a sixteenth-century chair is drawn up before what Berenson called its "impressive simplicity"; beyond, an elaborate Flemish tapestry, an *Adam and Eve* by a follower of Lucas Cranach, a doorway.

Giotto, says Vasari in *Lives of the Artists*, could draw a perfect circle freehand, and the artist's advances in representation were much admired in his day. This little fragment in Isabella's collection shows an emotional moment: four haloed (though solid) adults, with the holy baby indeed reaching for his mother—his Presentation in the Temple important in ecclesiastical and art history, but not to Him. Now, in the dimness of the Gothic Room I am here with Giotto's steady hand, on the Fenway in Boston, but also in my own more recent memories, among the stepped streets of Assisi...*tourists with prayer books, with guidebooks... The enormous basilica of San Francesco rises from the edge of a cliff, the air of Umbria spread out behind it, a slight haze in the blue green distance. Inside frescoes by Giotto cover the upper walls with episodes from the life of St. Francis, frescoes that crystallize the connection between art and religion in images of this young man of good family who couldn't figure out what to do in life and so became a saint.*[35] *Giotto's figures are solid, reassuring, clear. In the vast meeting place below them, monks are deconstructing in multiple languages the image of Francesco almost naked in the street, returning his clothes to his father, who is angry at the life choice his son has finally made. The gentle later image of Francis in the garden, his arms out to the birds, is sporadically lit by coin-operated illumination.* Here, too, in this room it is dim and shadowy, an impression of faith drawn freehand hovering among the murmuring visitors. As for Isabella at the pagoda in the Siamese jungle, the empty space around me, and around Giotto's imagined Presentation, fills with the impermanence and imperfection of my own vanished time, and of his.

Very Rich Cloth (with floral pattern)
French or Italian velvet (14c) in the Chapel

And Isabella? Oh yes... the showpiece in the room is of course the portrait of Isabella herself, before which a woman is protesting to her companion that she was sure the dress was red. This is very interesting to me, as was a fragment of conversation overheard in the Dutch Room on the floor below, where what is often most interesting to visitors is the daring of the theft, the scandalous absence, the continuing mystery of the lost paintings. But the two guys I tuned into as they wheeled through the place were discussing what one of them saw as an even cleverer theft. *Back in her day,* he said (as if high-level art chicanery no longer made headlines), *museums didn't bid*

---

35. The wabi-sabi of life—simultaneous devolution and evolution.

against each other, and she would get someone to front for her at the auctions, as if a museum were after the painting, and so they didn't bid against her and she'd get it cheap. What fun it is: the old gossip still the thrill here, the lady with the red dress on and the five-carat rubies on her slippers.

I am tired now. There is so much to see in this palace and so much time to absorb. Centuries of labor, of creation and dissolution. At the top of the stairs on the third floor I have been studying a tapestry woven in Flanders with a tumbling of literalized proverbs illustrated on it. A man actually falling between two stools, one biting a pillar (the hypocritical churchgoer), and somebody belling a real cat. The fingers that wove these witty and instructive images now 500 years still. On the second floor I suddenly notice that the railing at the head of the stairs is made of the head and foot of a seventeenth-century Italian bed. The center of the head has a haloed figure worked into it, crowning sleep, still watching over the vanished sleepers, and oblivious to me as I (by chance) am not to it. On a later visit I see for the first time in a corner at the far end of the Long Gallery a terra-cotta *Virgin and Child* kneeling together, the work of Matteo Civitali, "an unusually realistic and sentimental sculptor for his period" who, according to the 1935 *General Catalogue,* "nevertheless preserved the essential strength and sincerity of his Florentine background." I think again of the ritual of the museum, how much time is needed for this world to unfold, for this sincere quattrocentro Christian sweetness, in its shadowy position between two Botticelli paintings, to find me. And I think of those who do spend their days here, the guards especially, and of Okakura's wonder at the aesthetic stamina necessary to live among all this. The time and spirit art asks for, and offers.

2 Palace Road
The side entrance around the corner

Descending the stairs, I remember a young artist named Lee Mingwei, who in 2000 was briefly resident in Mrs. Gardner's carriage house while planning an installation for the museum. There is one display space within its walls that, like Hope from Pandora's box, escapes the strictures of Isabella's will. The loophole that allowed the dismantling of the Buddhist meditation room in 1971, today making space for the gift shop and a small café, has also allowed for a gallery where new and rotating exhibitions can be shown. Since 1992 the museum has had an artist-in-residence program that brings in annually five or six contemporary artists. Like a fragment of her biography refusing to lie in the grave with her, artists are still invited to Fenway Court "to reinvigorate the Museum through the work and presence of living artists."

Lingering in the spirit of the place, Mingwei served in the garden a beautifully prepared pasta at a small white table inside the ivy-covered walls. Conversation flowed, dusk fell, and so did a light rain, very light, as we sat on in an aura of hospitality and ease. We drank some wine. When it was time to leave, the friendly guards unlocked the door for us onto Palace Road—the secret door at the side, not the grand entrance to Isabella's pleasures—and we came out of what had seemed an enchanted space.

Lee was leaving shortly, his meditations there almost done, but the following year they took form as *The Living Room Project*, transforming the escaped space into a comfortable living room with an oriental rug, a couch, chairs, coffee table, lamps. Gesturing toward Mrs. Gardner's time were several large potted plants and a couple of hanging cages with colored songbirds in them. And then there was a rotating series of hosts, drawn mostly from the museum's staff, who brought in for two days each objects of their own—books, or photographs, or pieces of art—and received visitors there, offering tea and cookies and conversation, explaining why they had brought the objects and what they meant. It was not an enchanted space, but doing something the rest of the palazzo did not: it said, Please touch. The room said, Be part of the show. And, like Sophie Calle's *Last Seen . . .*, it put back into the space of display those who are living with Mrs. Gardner's art. The installation was trying to reimagine the absent presence of our hostess Isabella Gardner.

Lee Mingwei and Guests in *The Living Room* Project

Lee's work here was invoking her *fantôme*, the missing hospitality that drew toward her artists and friends and the curious social world of her time. Like Sophie Calle's transformations of image and text, Lee was asking us to notice something about art that often passes unnoticed: the relationship to it of the museum workers who live with it. They became briefly our hosts, the immediate bearers of the spirit that assembled the collection. The installation pulled visitors out of our contemporary anonymity, and briefly made us part of an intimate circle, like those who met the art when Isabella was alive. For a moment we ceased to be the public, and became part of a private world, a world whose revealing documents had not yet been burned.

The mingling of a nineteenth-century parlor with an ordinary living room brought out some of the contradictions of the Gardner Museum, as well as some of the pleasures we have in mingling past and present, participating in traditional behavior, dipping into it, seeing where it fits and doesn't fit. Lee Mingwei is from a pre-Revolutionary Taiwanese family; his own story is full of historical anachronism, and the pleasures, perhaps, of moving easily in several worlds, as art does, as we do when we give ourselves to it. His work here said, "Linger in the beautiful foolishness of things," be true to your individual taste. It said, Be here now, as art always is.

So this is my side entrance to Isabella Stewart Gardner. All we can know of her is the art she has left, and the sympathetic participation we can muster to let it achieve its effect. Her house is a terrifically American appropriation of European and Asian culture. That's what Calle's and Lee's work shows. The sympathy we have with their art, which is of and for our time and place, refracts into sympathy with Isabella's. It allows me to shake off her will, to wander as I please through the fragmentary documentation of her friendships, the indefinite versions of her life story, to move within the frame left empty by her death and make the place my own. Thus do I approach her, at the borders of nothingness where we are together.

Eight decades in the grave now, she is the necessary vacuum within this generous jumble, this testimony to a past world of plunder and pleasure, arrogance and aesthetic longing. My mind is now the canvas on which she paints, and her Fenway Court now a palimpsest for my tapestry of ladies stepping into the world, my folding screens of Oriental enchantment, my travel sketches and portraits of gentlemen in black, my serpentine and silver souvenirs of Egypt and Assisi, Istanbul, New York, my literary opinions and emptied teacups—a thousand trifles now ordered to my will and pleasure. The impermanence and imperfection of this inside-out Venetian palazzo has opened a psychic space for me, for my schizophrenic reading habits, for my own incomplete, impermanent, imperfect pleasure in her art.

* * *

Postscript: An Invitation to Tea
The making and sharing of a bowl of tea give
rise to a profound aesthetic experience

1

The iron kettle sighs like the wind in the pines

When Okakura Kakuzo died in 1913, Mrs. Gardner installed in a windowless chamber at the back of Fenway Court the meditation room to which she moved much of her Asian art. It was off limits to the public, a private space fitted like a Buddhist temple that held (among other artifacts) the tea implements – bowl, caddy, whisk, charcoal basket, etc.—given to her by her lost friend. Maud Elliott said the room was "rather awful in its dark thrill, like a tomb." Dismantled in 1971, the space once dedicated to Okakura's memory has freely evolved—as memory does, and art. The small gift shop and café are modern contrivances, but the plain empty gallery where the museum now shows contemporary art seems in the spirit of something the two friends shared: Okakura's encouragement of individual creativity within a traditional context and Isabella's continuing patronage of working artists. In 2003, the museum's centennial year, that gallery became a condensed—a Conceptual—version of the museum itself, the artist Joseph Kosuth having plundered from its walls some of the best paintings and from its cases of correspondence and memorabilia a number of letters. There, in early April, I found Isabella's grand conception extracted, reduced, surrounded by—engulfed by— fragments of history inscribed in copperplate script on the walls.

This experience came to me on the day I was searching through Mrs. Gardner's palazzo for works I had not closely examined, but whose names I had myself plundered for my own conception. Seeking the meaning of her memory palace, wanting the absent Isabella to start to life, experimenting with her aesthetic bowl of tea, I had lifted from the museum's catalogue the names of her possessions and used them to structure this literary exploration. Then the stolen language returned me to the scene of the crime, where I soon found myself crouching in a corner of the Blue Room to see the watercolor study called *Spirit of the Water Lily*, by John La Farge. La Farge was a friend of Isabella's, an innovative stained-glass artist and a successful painter in 1884 when Mrs. Gardner bought the little study. Two years later he traveled to Japan with Henry Adams. He became a close friend of Okakura Kakuzo. Another painting of a water lily he did is at the Museum of Fine Arts just up the Fenway.

2

Straw sandals as those worn by Zen monks are donned
through the tea garden

I had two catalogues to guide me around the Blue Room, for companionship in my scouting. The 1935 *General Catalogue* says this little study was for a design used in a book. The 1997 catalog (offered more modestly as *Guide to the Collection*) says it was painted in 1860/61 for a stained-glass window design, Mr. La Farge pondering the connection between this rather showy flower and its "spirit," apparently a slender female with little wings hovering in a graceful curve, her feet just touching the blossom. It seems an absurd image. Not what I had expected at all, having seen the water lily in the MFA, which has all the spirit it needs just floating above its own reflection, the yellow center presenting itself to the viewer among the open white petals. The literalness of the pretty fairy, I mean, is hard to take.

I hope the stained-glass window project didn't work out, and that the final disposition was simply as frontispiece in *Songs from the Old Dramatists*, 1873. The Old Dramatist who comes to mind is Shakespeare, whose fairies and spirits are a tuneful bunch, and most of them probably vain enough to be quite pleased with La Farge's colorful illustration. Anyway, I guess Mrs. G. liked it, although she didn't give it much prominence in her display—maybe by the time she was making her decisions about the Blue Room she found it less amusing than when she acquired it.

More prominent in the room is Howard Gardiner Cushing's painting called *The Shower of Gold*, a bright image of a woman's cascading hair lit by painted daylight from an open window. It's the artist's wife, in a romantic feminine moment. Across the room is Rosa Bonheur's *A She-Goat*, also having a feminine moment, lying at ease with her delicate legs and plump rump toward the viewer, her gender distinctly visible. You see how surprising it can be to be clear about the images that go with the words you've stolen; I was very glad to be lingering in this beautiful foolishness.

3

The subdued lighting and simple interior relax the mind, yet sharpen the senses

Thinking of *The Book of Tea*, I followed the clues from 1935 into the West Cloister, where I found a red marble holy water basin (in the far corner, and now in fact behind the information desk), and then looked as directed "diagonally opposite, on a column" to the marble statue of a woman representing Virtue, which on a more careful reading of my source turned out to be *a* Virtue. A Virtue is of course different from Virtue itself, and I have to admit more in keeping with the fragmentary nature of this museum and probably my own use of it as well. Also, by the way, for the Kosuth exhibit in the back room, which scatters fragments of cultural and biographical information among the selected splendid paintings. So, this Virtue I'm looking up at is small and pudding-faced with modest drapery, definitely a northern style Virtue—French Gothic form, says the catalogue, although probably done by an Italian—a tomb figure from fourteenth-century Naples that five hundred years on ends up in a shadowy corner in Boston.

In the Titian Room on the third floor I spotted the *Girl Taking a Thorn from Her Foot* right away. She's completely naked and apparently absorbed in her minor auto-surgical task, the result no doubt of running shoeless through the Renaissance landscape. The *General Catalogue* is moderately prolix here: the composition, it says, has a lineage that includes Dürer, Marcantonio, Marco da Ravenna, and finally Raphael's designs for decorating a bathroom for Cardinal Bibbiena in the Vatican.[36] In smaller type it mentions the work was purchased through Bernard (actually, it calls him Bernhard) Berenson as a work by Correggio. The *Guide* corrects Berenson, calling the painting *Venus Wounded by a Rose's Thorn*, and attributing it to an "unknown painter." It keeps some of the lineage, though—Marco da Ravenna, and Cardinal Bibbiena's *stufetto*—a bathing situation derived from Rome, well beyond what W. S. Bigelow offered President Roosevelt. Marco was killed in the Sack of Rome in 1527, but before that happened he made a careful study of Raphael's

---

36. Cardinal Bibbiena in return introduced Raphael to his niece, La Forinara, who became his most famous model.

first enthusiastic dive into full Roman style. *Derived from Raphael*, notes the little tag on the painting itself, stepping briskly away from the problem.

More disturbing than this transformation sixty years later of an ordinary Girl into Venus, with its unwelcome emphasis on the Thorn rather than the Foot, was the *fantôme* beside it, in the spot where I expected to find Francesco Torbido's *A Lady in a Turban*. This at least was an official museological *fantôme* and not more news about the 1990 theft, like the unpleasant reminder I'd had in the Short Gallery when I went to find Degas's *Leaving the Paddock*. (In order to touch that lost work I had to get on the Web later and find what Sophie Calle's informants had said. "My favorite was the jockey going into the race," said the clearest of her voices, "... roughly 4 x 6 inches, very detailed with a lot of buildings around and every brick individually painted...." Perhaps inevitably, another opinion was that the stolen Degas drawings "seemed like quick sketches that he almost dashed off on a napkin while he was having a glass of absinthe" – Degas himself out of the paddock and fooling around.) Torbido's *Lady*, at any rate—and to my relief— turned up as part of the Kosuth installation in the gallery on the first floor; it proved to be a large, brown-toned work, the turban sitting well back from the lady's appealing face. When Isabella Gardner bought it in 1896, Berenson told her it was a portrait of Isabella d'Este by a Venetian painter called Lanzani. Torbido was either Venetian or Veronese, depending on which catalogue you believe.

<h2 style="text-align:center">4</h2>

Every small item is appreciated for its subtle beauty

The most charming emergence from my catalogue texts was that *Young Lady of Fashion* by Paolo Uccello, in the Long Gallery. She's a fifteenth-century young lady, in profile, with a very high forehead and a long neck, and an embroidered cap from out the back of which falls a bit of blond hair, like a horse's tail. My *General Catalogue* says that Uccello was not seduced by his scientific researches in perspective and anatomy into a "too literal naturalism." That is, this lovely portrait is the idea of a well-turned out young lady and, appropriately, for forty-five dollars its likeness can be purchased in the gift shop as part of a slender gold-framed mirror.

So I continued, hunting down the *Very Rich Cloth* in the chapel and the Japanese screens in the elevator passages—one of them practically invisible, unlit, in a reflective, glass-fronted cabinet. Chinese gentlemen (or *literati*, 1935) are occupying themselves (or *relaxing*, again 1935) with music and wine by a mountain stream, a tantalizing glimpse into a seventeenth-century moment had it not been consigned to this dark space, moved (or evolving) from the privacy of the Buddhist meditation room by Morris Carter three years after his Dea's death. The *Chrysanthemums and Orchids...* on the floor below were easier to see, the elaborate gold tracing catching what light there was. In the courtyard once more the cascading nasturtiums were hung from the third-floor windows, spilling down high above the azaleas and orchids and potted orange trees, the splashing fountain, the *Granite Hawk of Horus*, the soft light of the unseasonably frosty day.

Finally I went to study the conceptual art in the back gallery, where Kosuth, as part of the museum's Artist-in-Residence program, had made his own sense of the collection, of the phenomenon of Isabella's will. *Art speaks of the relations between people*, Kosuth has said, *and between objects within a context*. The context in this case was multiple: the empty gallery, the museum surrounding it, the collecting habits of Isabella's time, and her relationships with its artists and collectors. And then there was my time, and me with my own purposes here, and the other visitors in the room, another fragment of my encounter, my own production of meaning, of this subtle and unexpected beauty.

Like me, Kosuth has made free with the treasures of the place, mining the past for its disjunctions and felicities, its scraps of lives, what he calls *attic residue*, those *items which bridge the detritus of cultural production with the fragments of social intercourse*, as he calls them. Some of his bridging fragments are letters he extracted from their glass cases found throughout the building and hung among the art and his elegantly transcribed slices of text. People like Isabella Gardner and Bernard Berenson and Henry James and Corinna Smith wrote letters every day, short notes on folded paper—scrawling handwriting and sympathetic phrasings. They checked the post several times a day the way we check our e-mail, and so kept up with each other across town and across the Atlantic. From those glass cases in Isabella's carefully constructed rooms Kosuth heard what he calls the *sottovoce murmur*, the subtitles to the great images on the walls. Their historical testimony punctuates the larger text of the art, he says. His work here is keeping up with Mrs. Gardner across time, drawing the past close, making it present. The reality of the lost Isabella is both then and now, in these objects and elsewhere, something to be seen only as I move around the room.

5

Delicate flowers, picked at dawn, represent nature

Kosuth has also extracted from the collection some of its most delightful works: Holbein's *Lady Butts*, Masaccio's *Young Man in a Scarlet Turban*, that *Woman in Green and Crimson* by Pollaiuolo that I love, a Pinturicchio *Virgin and Child*, two leaves from Arabic manuscripts, formerly undiscoverable in the gloom of the Tapestry Room. It's wonderful to see them here, to have them lit up in the gallery's full illumination and by Kosuth's patiently transcribed texts all over the walls.

Around the bottom of the room run in two long lines instructions from an 1872 book of etiquette. I circled the room, reading about order of precedence for going in to dinner, the relative rankings of clergy and aristocracy, what to do with your napkin, how to eat salmon and turbot, or soup. I am told to remove my gloves and put them on my lap, and never to let a knife anywhere near my mouth. It's the art of social intercourse, the aesthetics of the dinner party, a vanished spirit still hovering over Fenway Court. Like Berenson's connoisseurship, the gestures described in this text that guided me twice around the gallery's perimeter define value, importance, and identity. Are you a Rembrandt or a Flinck? From Venice or Verona? A follower of Correggio or Raphael? Are you a Young Lady of Fashion? A Woman Representing Virtue, *a* Virtue? How you handle your knife or your cherry tart is full of meaning.

Around the top of the walls Kosuth had inscribed a time-line of cultural and historical events. Political revolutions and bobbed hair, Chaplin's million-dollar salary, and outbreaks of disease. And between top and bottom, running among the old artworks, is a fragmentary history twining Gardner and Berenson and James McNeill Whistler. Whistler is the artist with an agenda for the future, Berenson the historian with an agenda for the past; Isabella Gardner runs between them, the collector with an agenda for her present pleasure. Kosuth has projected onto the walls a history of their relationships, his own collection of moments from their biographies: the sale to Mrs. Gardner of the Pinturicchio for three times what Mary Berenson had hoped to get for it; Whistler's legal triumph in the matter of Lady Eden's portrait; Isabella firing the Italian floor-layers for imitating her. He sends me around the walls again and again, my own agenda folding into his contexts. We take from the past what pleases us and make it our own.

6

The whisk is deftly raised from the bowl . . . the tea is ready

Kosuth's one room asks for time and patience as seriously as Mrs. Gardner's palazzo-sized work. Only, here under the bright lights, the art and its setting are not protected from your sympathetic and corrosive gaze. To find the patterns, to understand how all this white copperplate script on the blue-painted walls connects to the visual art in the museum is an unfolding of experience, just as the rooms upstairs open and open into each other: Early Italian into Raphael into Short Gallery, or Veronese into Titian into Long Gallery into Chapel. The tea-master has prepared something special for you to share, something to sharpen your senses. You are invited to linger; your mind becomes part of the art.

One family group was wondering aloud who Bernard Berenson was, and I explained as best I could, hurriedly, while we stared at each other, hopeful strangers among the art. My own collaboration with Isabella's project now includes this brief relationship, as well as the voice of another woman who said impatiently she hadn't time to read all this. (Indeed; our time on earth is short.) The guard stood at the entrance clicking his counter and watching to see the space didn't get too crowded. Visitors came and went while I explored the walls. People read in snatches, in puzzlement, in pleasure, curious, hungry, moving on to the café or the gift shop.

This installation said "please touch" in a very different language from Lee Mingwei's. In this space Isabella was not so hospitable; she separates from her objects, becomes one of her own curiosities, a work of art requiring connoisseurship to find, skill to properly install. This means you may have to crouch down to see her, or crane your neck. She depends on your patience, waiting for your mind to let her paint on its canvas, as Kosuth has done. Like the great Titian painting hanging near the Bellini Christ and the swath of silk from the green party dress, context has been mingled into the art. The outside world has entered here in the living room. Roaming the museum in search of the art that completes my own text, I am at home walking around this roomful of writing. I am no longer oarless among these fragments of time and history. *The tea-master,* says Okakura, *held that real appreciation of art is only possible to those who make of it a living influence.* Invited, I linger and linger in this ephemeral space. The masterpiece is of ourselves, as we are of the masterpiece.

Notes

8   "refute some of the legends"; Morris Carter, *Isabella Stewart Gardner and Fenway Court* (Boston: Houghton Mifflin, 1925), p. viii.

"without being utterly"; Carter, p. 234.

11   "in a voice like a parrot"; Tharp, p. 345.

11n   "Lithuanian..."; Louise Hall Tharp, *Mrs. Jack: A Biography of Isabella Stewart Gardner* (Boston: Little Brown, 1965), p. 129.

12n   "Sitting in the rich gloom"; Joseph Lindon Smith, unpublished letter, ISGM archives.

"the perfect type"; Corinna Lindon Smith, *Interesting People: Eighty Years with the Great and Near-Great* (Norman, OK: University of Oklahoma Press, 1962), p. 303.
"plain soldiers..."; C. L. Smith, p. 308.

14   "a performative mode"; Wanda Corn, "Art Matronage in Post-Victorian America" in *Fenway Court XXVII* (Boston: Trustees of the Isabella Stewart Gardner Museum, 1995), p. 13.

"Battles are rarely"; C.L. Smith, p. 314.

15   "dog of a Christian"; C.L. Smith, p. 226.

19 "Do you remember"; Maud Howe Elliott, *Three Generations* (Boston: Little Brown, 1924), p. 273.

   "an enviable distinction"; Elliott, p. 338.

20n "little school teacher"; C.L. Smith, p. 167.

21 "in the presence"; Eugenia Kaledin, *The Education of Mrs. Henry Adams* (Philadelphia: Temple University Press, 1981), p. 95.

   "alas, I fear"; Henry Adams, *The Letters of Henry Adams*, ed. Levenson et al., (Cambridge: Harvard University Press, 1982), Vol. II, p. 133.

23 "the lowest of Dante's"; Marian Hooper Adams, *The Letters of Mrs. Henry Adams*, ed. Ward Thoron (Boston: Little, Brown, 1936), p. 167.

   "not only fills"; M.H. Adams, p. 183.

23n "Henry says,"; M.H. Adams, p.224

24 "Down come an elderly"; M.H. Adams, p. 159.

   "We never dine"; M.H. Adams, p. 182.

25 "mouse in picture shops"; M.H. Adams, p. 182.

26   "a perfect Voltaire"; Kaledin, p. 166.

           "how fond of her"; Tharp, p. 272.

28   "the world knows"; Kaledin, p. 46.

           "on the theory"; Kaledin, p. 168.

31   "a dinner of garlic"; M.H. Adams, p. 210.

31n   "Why is the coffee"; Elliott, p. 379.

34   "the truth of things"; Henry James, *The Portrait of a Lady* (New York: W.W. Norton, 1995), p. 465.

37   "Pray, who undressed you?"; Tharp, p. 43.

41   "an instinct for social freedom"; Douglass Shand-Tucci, *The Art of Scandal: The Life and Times of Isabella Stewart Gardner* (New York: Harper Collins, 1997), p. 123.

           "the extraordinary fineness"; quoted in Shand-Tucci, p. 77.

42   "a brilliant example"; Shand-Tucci, p. 277.

           "a dialogue between"; Shand-Tucci, p. 230.

           "persuaded works of art"; Shand-Tucci, p. 231.

42n   "Deeply, passionately"; Shand-Tucci, p. 51.

47   "life of cultured luxury"; Barbara Strachey and Jayne Samuels, *Mary Berenson: A Self-Portrait from Her Diaries and Letters* (New York: W.W. Norton, 1983), p. 58.

48   "the very rare and wonderful"; Bernard Berenson and Isabella Stewart Gardner, *The Letters of Bernard Berenson and Isabella Stewart Gardner*, ed. Rollin Van N. Hadley (Boston: Northeastern University Press, 1987), pp. 94-95.

50   "Prince on Horseback"; Yasuko Horioka, *The Life of Kakuzo, Author of "The Book of Tea"* (Tokyo: The Hokuseido Press, 1963), p. 31.

51   "true beauty could only"; Okakura Kakuzo, *The Book of Tea* (New York and Tokyo: Kodansha, 1989), p. 89.

       "linger in the beautiful"; Okakura, p. 40.

52   "positioned himself"; Anne Nishimura Morse in *Okakura Tenshin and the Museum of Fine Arts* (Nagoya: Nagoya Bosutan Bijutsukan, 1999), p. 46.

       "Our mind is the canvas"; Okakura, p. 97.

       "creases like the leathern"; Okakura, p. 47.

53 "a worship of the imperfect"; Okakura, p. 29.

    "Perhaps tomorrow night"; Berenson and Gardner, p. 342.

    "At last we really care"; Strachey and Samuels, p. 194.

    "The stars have dissolved"; quoted in Shand-Tucci, p. 262.

58n "speculated that Buddhism"; Christopher Benfey, *The Great Wave: Gilded Age Misfits, Japanese Eccentrics, and the Opening of Old Japan* (New York: Random House, 2003), p. 62.

60 "pigeons whirring"; Carter, p. 64.

    "It was two days there"; Carter, p. 60.

    "wonderful stories"; Carter, p. 71.

61 "all alone…"; Carter, p. 81.

64 "Japan was a charming"; Lawrence W. Chisolm, *Fenollosa: The Far East and American Culture* (New Haven: Yale University Press, 1963), p. 120.

65 "Professor Fenollosa"; M. Fenollosa in Ernest Francisco Fenollosa, *Epochs of Chinese and Japanese Art* (New York: Yamanaka, 1907), p. xx.

65   "studying, acquiring"; M. Fenollosa in E.F. Fenollosa, p. xxi.

66   "those qualities"; Benfey, p. 273.

66n   "It was the rosy"; Mary Fenollosa, *Blossoms From a Japanese Garden* (New York: Frederick A. Stokes, 1913), p. 8.

68   "Japan was swarming"; Bigelow in Seiichi Yamaguchi, *On and After the Death of Ernest F. Fenollosa: Viewed Chiefly through the Correspondence between Mrs. Fenollosa and Charles Lang Freer* (Reprinted from the Saitama daigaku kiyÿ, Jimbun kagaku hen, no. 25, 1976. p. 17-65), p. 64.

69n   "please report me"; William Sturgis Bigelow, *The Selected Letters of Dr. William Sturgis Bigelow*, ed. Akiko Murakata (unpublished thesis, 1971), p. 84.

71   "a bathroom with sun"; Bigelow, p. 278.

72   "The art of life"; Okakura, p. 64.

72n   "vain, meddlesome"; Bigelow, unpublished letter, ISGM archives.

        "it was good"; Bigelow, unpublished letter, ISGM archives.

75   "*genuine* Gothic"; Berenson and Gardner, p. 199-200.

"a natural itinerary"; Gilbert Wendel Longstreet, *The Isabella Stewart Gardner Museum General Catalogue* (Boston: Trustees of the Isabella Stewart Gardner Museum, 1935), p. 14.

76   "an orgy"; Berenson and Gardner, p. 66.

77   "she has adorers"; Berenson and Gardner, p. 65.

"can be a ribald"; Hilliard T. Goldfarb, *The Isabella Stewart Gardner Museum: A Companion Guide and History* (New Haven: Yale University Press, 1995), p. 118.

86   "or do some banging"; Carter, p. 69.

87   "that disposition"; Jane Austen, *Persuasion* (London and New York: Penguin Books, 1998), p. 147.

88   "Nothing he ever wrote"; Elliott, p. 196.

"rapidly moving narrative"; John Pilkington, Jr., *Francis Marion Crawford* (New York: Twayne, 1964), p. 191.

"What you tell me"; Pilkington, p. 103.

90   "well-known in Rome"; Francis Marion Crawford, *To Leeward* (New York and Boston: Macmillan, 1884), p. 404.

90   "found means to"; Crawford, p. 44.

            "strong and radiantly"; Crawford, p. 45.

91n   "She lived"; Pilkington, p. 46.

            "someone else's work"; Pilkington, p. 48.

92n   "My lady late"; Shand-Tucci, p. 50.

97   "Limitless indeed"; Okakura, p. 88.

98   "They want the costly"; Okakura, p. 103.

            "This faint evidence"; Leonard Koren, *Wabi-Sabi for Artists,
            Designers, Poets & Philosophers* (Berkeley: Stone Bridge Press,
            1994), p. 42.

99   "nothingness itself"; Koren, p. 45.

100   "In vacuum alone"; Okakura, p. 66.

101   "the exact opposite"; Koren, p. 50.

            "The Abode of Shadow"; Berenson and Gardner, p. 370.

104n   "Think of being the victim"; Adams, Vol. III, p. 251.

105   "secret understanding"; Okakura, p. 98.

111   "Then look how delicately"; Berenson and Gardner, p. 202.

113   "an unusually realistic"; Longstreet, p. 233.

117   "rather awful"; Elliott, p. 377.

122   "Art speaks of the relations"; Joseph Kosuth, *No Thing, No Self, No Form, No Principle (Was Certain)*, ed. Renate Damsch-Wiehager (Stuttgart: Edition Cantz, 1993), p. 11.

126   "The tea-master"; Okakura, p. 127.

[The headings in the Postscript reproduce the captions for the illustrations (photographs by Takao Inoue) in *The Book of Tea* by Okakura Kakuzo (New York: Kodansha International, 1991).]

Further Acknowledgments

Henry Adams, *The Education of Henry Adams* (Boston: Houghton Mifflin, 1974).

E. Digby Baltzell, *Puritan Boston and Quaker Philadelphia: Two Protestant Ethics and the Spirit of Class Authority* (New York: Free Press, 1979).

Bainbridge Bunting, *Houses of Boston's Back Bay* (Cambridge: Harvard University Press, 1967).

Francis Marion Crawford, *Mr. Isaacs* (New York: Macmillan, 1909).

Paul DiMaggio, "Cultural Entrepreneurship in Nineteenth-Century Boston: The Creation of an Organizational Base for High Culture in America" in *Media, Culture and Society: A Critical Reader* (London and Beverly Hills:, Sage Publications, 1986).

Ann Douglas, *The Feminization of American Culture* (New York: Farrar Straus and Giroux, 1998).

Betty G. Farrell, *Elite Families: Class and Power in Nineteenth-Century Boston* (Albany: SUNY Press, 1993).

Otto Friedrich, *Clover* (New York: Simon and Schuster, 1979).

Lyndall Gordon, *A Private Life of Henry James* (New York: W.W. Norton, 1998).

Martin Green, *The Mount Vernon Street Warrens: A Boston Story 1860–1910* (New York: Scribners, 1989).

Henry James, *Letters from the Palazzo Barbaro*, ed., Rosella Mamoli Zorzi (London, Pushkin Press, 1998).

Lee Mingwei, *The Living Room* (Boston: The Isabella Stewart Gardner Museum, 2000).

Lawrence W. Levine, *Highbrow/Lowbrow: The Emergence of Cultural Hierarchy in America* (Cambridge: Harvard University Press, 1988).

Kathleen C. McCarthy, *Women's Culture: American Philanthropy and Art, 1830–1930* (Chicago: University of Chicago Press, 1991).

Patricia O'Toole, *The Five of Hearts: An Intimate Portrait of Henry Adams and His Friends, 1880–1918* (New York: C. N. Potter, 1990).

Aline Saarinen, *The Proud Possessors: The Lives, Times and Tastes of Some Adventurous American Art Collectors* (New York: Random House, 1958).

Ernest Mason Satow and A.G.S. Hawes, *Handbook for Travellers in Central and Northern Japan* (London: Murray, 1884).

Ronald Story, *The Forging of an Aristocracy: Harvard and the Boston Upper Class 1800–1870* (Middletown: Wesleyan University Press, 1980).

Gore Vidal, "The Political Novel from Darius the Great to President Chester Arthur" in *Il Magnifico Crawford*, ed. Gordon Poole (Sant'Agnello, Italy: Acts of the International Conference, 1990).

Siegfried Wichmann, *Japonisme: The Japanese Influence on Western Art Since 1858* (New York: Thames & Hudson, 1999).

CREDITS

Page 59   Edward Sylvester Morse at Yokohama. © Peabody Essex
             Museum 2006.

Page 63   American Consul in Japan. © Peabody Essex Museum
             2006.

Page 70   Attributed to: Kobayashi Eitaku,Japanese, 1843–1890.
             Portrait of W. S. Bigelow. Japanese, Meiji era, 1870s–
             1880s, Hanging scroll; ink on silk. Image: 56.7 x 41.6
             cm (22 $^5/_{16}$ x 16 $^3/_8$ in.) Overall: 143 x 59.6 cm (56 $^5/_{16}$ x
             23 $^7/_{16}$ in.), William Sturgis Bigelow Collection,
             11.9221. © 2007 Museum of Fine Arts, Boston.

Page 74   The Chinese Room at Fenway Court. Isabella Stewart
             Gardner Museum, Boston.

Page 80   *Birthday Portrait of a Lady.* Chinese, Qing dynasty, late
             18th century. Ink, color and gold on silk. 236.9 x 124.5
             cm (93 $^1/_4$ x 49 in.), Marshall H. Gould Fund, 2000.976.
             © 2007 Museum of Fine Arts, Boston.

Page 81   John Singer Sargent, Isabella Stewart Gardner, 1888.
             Isabella Stewart Gardner Museum, Boston.

Page 84   John Singer Sargent, *Mrs. Gardner in White*, 1922.
             Isabella Stewart Gardner Museum, Boston.

The Author

Patricia Vigderman grew up in Washington, D.C. and Europe. She graduated from Vassar College, after which a circuitous course led her through editing, translating, free-lance journalism, teaching, marriage, motherhood, divorce, a doctoral dissertation (on nineteenth-century novels as film, as history, and as autobiography), and a lot of time in museums. Her recent writing has appeared in *Georgia Review, Harvard Review, Iowa Review, Kenyon Review, Mid-American Review, Northwest Review, Raritan, Seneca Review*, and *Southwest Review*. She divides her year between Cambridge, Massachusetts and Gambier, Ohio, where she teaches in the English department at Kenyon College. She is married to the writer Lewis Hyde.

Marcella Hackbardt